What's Your Opera I.Q.?

What's Your OPERA I.Q.?

A QUIZ BOOK FOR OPERA LOVERS

Iris Bass

A Citadel Press Book
Published by Carol Publishing Group

A Citadel Press Book
Published by Carol Publishing Group

Citadel Press is a registered trademark of Carol Communications, Inc.

Editorial Offices: 600 Madison Avenue, New York, N.Y. 10022
Sales & Distribution Offices: 120 Enterprise Avenue, Secaucus, N.J. 07094
In Canada: Musson Book Company, a division of General Publishing Co., Ltd., Don Mills, Ontario

Queries regarding rights and permission should be addressed to Carol Publishing Group, 600 Madison Avenue, New York, N.Y. 10022

Carol Publishing Group books are available at special discounts for bulk purchases, for sales promotions, fund raising, or educational purposes. Special editions can be created to specifications. For details contact: Special Sales Department, Carol Publishing Group, 120 Enterprise Avenue, Secaucus, N.J. 07094

Manufactured in the United States of America

10 9 8 7 6 5 4 3 2 1

Library of Congress Cataloging-in-Publication Data

Bass, Iris.
    What's your opera I.Q.? / Iris Bass.
        p.   cm.
    "A Citadel Press book."
    ISBN 0-8065-1211-3
    1. Opera--Miscellanea. I. Title.
ML1700.B17   1991
782.1--dc20   91-7538
                                        CIP

TO ONE OF THE ANSWERS.
TO ALL OF THEM.

Introduction

THERE EXISTS an entire generation of operagoers not raised on the old Met and Maria Callas—people to whom listening to even an LP has become as outmoded as playing an Edison cylinder recording. Yet opera is far from a dead art. The multitude of rising stars, flourishing troupes (over seventy-five in New York City alone!), innovative stagings, and new works all demonstrate a vigorous continuation of this art form. Via compact discs, live recordings, simulcasts, videocassettes, and subtitled performances, audiences are now able to experience opera more fully than any previous generation. And though derided even in our own century as being too young a culture to be able to compete in the international music world, America is now holding its own on opera stages around the globe.

Written with a particular view toward what has been happening in the last two decades, *What's Your Opera I.Q.?* encompasses an eclectic repertoire that ranges from our rediscovery of Handel and bel canto composers to our "bread and butter" traditional favorites to our acceptance of "crossover" musicals and the works of modern American composers. Sources of this quiz material include current reference books such as the 1976 *Who's Who in Opera* and *The Concise Oxford Dictionary of Opera*, recent biographies of music personalities, libretti of hundreds of works being performed and recorded by contemporary artists, issues of *Opera News* covering the last ten years of productions worldwide, and the author's own attendance at live performances dating back to her first in-theater opera in 1971.

What's Your Opera I.Q.? brings readers up to date on black opera history; telecasts, films, and books are given their due; and U.S. regional companies and summer festivals are also represented. While the book does contain items about the Met's past, it also looks forward to things to come, with questions already derived from repertoire of that institution's postcentennial years. Meant to be instructional as well as fun, *What's Your Opera I.Q.?* is a detailed, scrupulously researched, yet lighthearted—even irreverant—celebration of the vitality and madness of opera.

Author's Note

(An Apology to Tchaikovsky *et al.*)

MANY OF THESE QUIZZES were created by working with standard editions of opera libretti—that is, from the original language portion of them. As operagoers are ever-distressed to learn, when texts are translated into English, whether for performance purposes or simple understanding, data such as numbers and object names may be changed in order to fit rhyme or meter. Also, idiomatic foreign expressions may be adjusted drastically to make sense in idiomatic English. Furthermore, English translations vary from edition to edition: one may have to make do with archaic poetic nonsense or may just as easily come upon a libretto that has been tailored to suit a specific modern staging. What's a quiz writer to do? For the sake of consistency and accuracy, I have gone to the original language of French, German, Italian, and Spanish operatic works when writing quizzes based upon their texts.

Because I cannot read Czech, Russian, or other Eastern languages, and cannot quite trust English translations of them for the above reasons, such operas do not appear in quizzes that require a fine knowledge of the wording of such libretti. Meanwhile, I have taken care to include many modern American and British works that I feel have gotten short shrift in other quiz books.

In choosing what works will be included overall, I have gone by the following definition: an opera is a vocal musical and dramatic work performed in an opera house. Thus, this book encompasses not only opera but also operetta and crossover musical comedies. A list of all works mentioned in the book appears as an appendix.

I hope that these quizzes will inspire their readers to explore the intricacies of this fascinating art form for themselves, in all its visual and aural glory. After the bits and pieces have provided you with hours of enjoyable mental gymnastics, do pursue the entire original sources for even greater pleasure!

What's Your Opera I.Q.?

Questions

1. BLUE BLOOD

Can you name the composers of the following operatic works?

1. *Le Roi d'Ys*
2. *L'Amore dei Tre Re*
3. *The King Goes Forth to France*
4. *Anna Bolena*
5. *Le Roi Malgré Lui*
6. *Elisabetta, Regina d'Inghilterra*
7. *A Life for the Tsar*
8. *Mary Queen of Scots*
9. *Le Roi l'A Dit*
10. *Ivan IV*
11. *The Tsar's Bride*
12. *Konigskinder*
13. *Le Roi de Lahore*
14. *Henry VIII*
15. *La Reine de Saba*

Extra Credit:

A. Of what country does Eurydice's guard claim he was once king, in *Orphée aux Enfers*?

B. Beverly Sills performed the roles of six queens with New York City Opera. What were they?

C. What is the name of Verdi's only comic opera aside from *Falstaff*?

2. DOUBLE ENTENDRES

While representing, in all cases, totally different characters, the character names listed at left each crop up in *two* operas listed at right (some popular names appear in even more works not listed here as choices). Can you match each name to two operas?

1. Elvira	a. *Mefistofele*
2. Leonora	b. *Luisa Miller*
3. Arturo	c. *Lucia di Lammermoor*
4. Lindoro	d. *Werther*
5. Amelia	e. *Il Barbiere di Siviglia*
6. Susanna	f. *La Forza del Destino*
7. Marcellina	g. *L'Italiana in Algeri*
8. Paolo	h. *Un Ballo in Maschera*
9. Ferrando	i. *Francesca di Rimini*
10. Marie	j. *La Fille du Régiment*
11. Tonio	k. *I Puritani*
12. Sophie	l. *Khovanshchina*
13. Rodolfo	m. *Così Fan Tutte*
14. Andrei	n. *Wozzeck*
15. Enrico	o. *Simon Boccanegra*
	p. *Pagliacci*
	q. *Fidelio*
	r. *Der Rosenkavalier*
	s. *Le Nozze di Figaro*
	t. *La Bohème*
	u. *Il Trovatore*
	v. *War and Peace*

Extra Credit:

Match each composer at left to his opera at right.

A. Richard Strauss	i. *Drei Waltzer*
B. Johann Strauss II	ii. *Padmâvati*
C. Oscar Straus	iii. *Les Indes Galantes*
D. Jean-Jacques Rousseau	iv. *Die Schweigsame Frau*
E. Albert Roussel	v. *Le Devin du Village*
F. Jean-Philippe Rameau	vi. *Der Zigeunerbaron*

3. TRIPLETS

Match each name at left to the opera the character appears in, at right.

1. Adina		a.	*Gianni Schicchi*
2. Amina		b.	*Il Turco in Italia*
3. Annina		c.	*L'Amore dei Tre Re*
4. Paquillo		d.	*La Sonnambula*
5. Pedrillo		e.	*L'Elisir d'Amore*
6. Pinellino		f.	*Der Rosenkavalier*
7. Fiorilla		g.	*L'Incoronazione di Poppea*
8. Fiora		h.	*La Finta Giardiniera*
9. Fiordiligi		i.	*Die Entführung aus dem Serail*
10. Belfiore		j.	*La Périchole*
11. Belcore		k.	*Don Giovanni*
12. Bemonte		l.	*La Traviata*
13. Ottavio		m.	*Così Fan Tutte*
14. Octavian			
15. Ottavia			

Extra Credit:

And to make each a quartet, match the following characters to their operas:

A. Aminta	i.	*Fidelio*
B. Pizaro	ii.	*Dido and Aeneas*
C. Florinda	iii.	*Die Schweigsame Frau*
D. Belinda	iv.	*L'Incoronazione di Poppea*
E. Ottone	v.	*Le Donne Curiose*

4. OOPS!

The answer to this quiz is simple, if you know your opera history. What do the following works have in common?

1. *La Traviata*
2. Rossini's *Il Barbiere di Siviglia*
3. *Carmen*
4. *Edgar*
5. *Tristan und Isolde*
6. *Julien*
7. *A Midsummer Marriage*
8. *Mefistofele*
9. *Guntram*
10. *Beatrice di Tenda*

Extra Credit:

What opera, which premiered at the Met in 1962, is unperformable today as a complete work, and why?

5. SIBLING RIVALRY

Can you match the operatic characters at left to their brothers and sisters at right?

1. Gualtiero	a. Zdenka
2. Lucia	b. Olga
3. Fiordiligi	c. Thisbe
4. Charlotte	d. Siegrune
5. Cunegonde	e. Lord Rochefort
6. Sieglinde	f. Tolomeo
7. Feodor	g. Giorgio
8. Arabella	h. Dorabella
9. Woglinde	i. Enrico
10. Tatiana	j. Xenia
11. Cleopatra	k. Dorothée
12. Clorinda	l. Sparafucile
13. Noémie	m. Siegmund
14. Anna Bolena	n. Sophie
15. Maddalena	o. Maximilian

Extra Credit:

A. What is the relationship of Steva and Laca in *Jenufa* (or, similarly, Wenzel and Hans in *The Bartered Bride*)?

B. In *Robert le Diable*, how are Alice and the title character related?

C. How does the bel canto opera *Crispino e lo Comare* relate to this quiz?

6. OTHER VOICES, OTHER ROOMS

The lines at left are traditionally performed offstage. Can you match them to their operas? For extra credit, identify their situations.

1. "A una fonta afflitto . . ."
2. "Momus, Momus, Momus, Zitti e discreti andiamoscene via"
3. "Magnificat anima mea Dominum"
4. "Vi fido"
5. "Zurück!"
6. "O Lola, ch'ai di latti la commisa"
7. "Largo al quadrupede sir della testa"
8. "Gittata i palisciemi"
9. "Ave Signor degli angelle del santi"
10. "Sauvee!"
11. "Jesu, vient de naitre . . ."
12. "De mon amie, Fleur endormie"
13. "Blanche Dourga . . ."
14. "Circe, Circe, kannst du mich horen?"
15. "Glou! glou! glou!"

a. Tosca
b. La Traviata
c. Les Contes d'Hoffmann
d. Werther
e. La Bohème
f. Cavalleria Rusticana
g. Ariadne auf Naxos
h. Manon
i. Faust
j. Les Pêcheurs de Perles
k. I Puritani
l. Otello
m. Lakmé
n. Mefistofele
o. Die Zauberflöte

7. NOMS DE TUNE

Twenty opera singers began their lives with the following
names. Can you guess their stage names?

An older generation

1. Rose Ponzillo
2. Maria Kalogeropoulou
3. Jacob Perelmuth
4. Rose Calvet
5. Helen Mitchell
6. Reba Fiersohn
7. Louise Beatty
8. George Burnson
9. Ernst Seiffert
10. Ernestine Rossier

Current artists

11. Cologero Anthony
    Caruso
12. Stientje Engel
13. Myra Beth Genis
14. Victoria Lopez
15. Alfredo Trujillo
16. Susan Dowell
17. Morris Miller
18. Gerard Tisserand
19. Alan Jones
20. Lillian Joyce Mallicky

Extra Credit:

A. Which director's name is really Gian Franco Corsi?

B. Which librettist began life as Emmanuel Conegliano?

C. What was Titta Ruffo's real name?

8. THE POWER OF THE PEN

Below, a list of popular operas. What do they have in common regarding their libretti?

1. *Intermezzo*
2. *Trouble in Tahiti*
3. *Mefistofele*
4. *Louise*
5. *Wozzeck*
6. *Carmina Burana*
7. *Les Troyens*
8. *Jenufa*
9. *Tristan und Isolde*
10. *The Medium*
11. *Pagliacci*

12. *Russalka*
13. *A Midsummer Marriage*
14. *The Gambler*
15. *Susannah*

Extra Credit:

A. What famous novelist wrote the libretto of *L'Enfant et les Sortilèges*?

B. What famous stage and film director created the libretto of Barber's *Antony and Cleopatra*?

C. What famous tenor co-authored the libretto of *A Midsummer Night's Dream*?

9. THE CHILDREN'S ARIA

"Children should be seen and not heard" goes the familiar saying. While some of the following are indeed mute parts, the pint-sized characters described here all have names. What are they?

1. The little blackamoor in *Der Rosenkavalier*.
2. The Tabor child "renamed" by William Jennings Bryan in *The Ballad of Baby Doe*.
3. Emile de Becque's son in *South Pacific*.
4. Boris Godunov's young son in *Boris Godunov*.
5. Guillaume Tell's young son in *Guillaume Tell*.
6. Juana's little girl in *La Loca*.
7. Gherardo and Nella's child in *Gianni Schicchi*.
8. The little boy in *Albert Herring*.
9. The young hero of *Where the Wild Things Are*.
10. Rose's kid brother in *Street Scene*.

Extra Credit:

What are the names of the Bailiff's eight children, in *Werther*?

10. MOONLIGHTING

The composers at left are now more famous for their instrumental works or conducting, but each man also wrote at least one opera—in fact, Vivaldi penned over forty, and Scarlatti some 115! Can you match each work at right to its composer?

1. Liszt	a. *Genoveva*
2. Ravel	b. *L'Enfant et les Sortilèges*
3. Schubert	c. *At the Boar's Head*
4. Scarlatti	d. *Le Plège de Méduse*
5. Fauré	e. *The Tender Land*
6. Walton	f. *Hin und Zurück*
7. Vivaldi	g. *Don Sanche*
8. Holst	h. *Fierrabras*
9. Copland	i. *The Nose*
10. Schumann	j. *Aleko*
11. Satie	k. *Pénélope*
12. Vaughan Williams	l. *Montezuma*
13. Shostakovich	m. *Troilus and Cressida*
14. Rachmaninov	n. *The Pilgrim's Progress*
15. Hindemith	o. *Mitridate Eupatore*

Extra Credit:

A. Four of "The Five" Russian composers wrote operas. Match each man to his respective work.

I. Borodin	i. *The Saracen*
II. Moussorgsky	ii. *Sadko*
III. Cui	iii. *Prince Igor*
IV. Rimsky-Korsakov	iv. *Khovanshchina*

B. Four of "Les Six" French composers also wrote operas. Match them.

V. Auric	v. *Jeanne d'Arc au Bucher*
VI. Honegger	vi. *Les Malheurs d'Orphée*
VII. Milhaud	vii. *La Voix Humaine*
VIII. Poulenc	viii. *Sous le Masque*

11. THE MAN BEHIND THE MYTH

The original ideas for some operatic plots trace all the way back to Ancient Greece. Can you name the people whose epic dramas, stories, and poems form the basis of the following works? (Example: the man behind *Dido and Aeneas* was Virgil.)

1. *Elektra*
2. *Alceste*
3. *L'Incoronzione di Poppea*
4. *King Priam*
5. *Les Troyens*
6. *Iphigénie en Tauride*
7. *Daphne*
8. *Medée*
9. *Philémon et Baucis*
10. *Oedipus Rex*

Extra Credit:

A. Metamorphoses occur in several operas. What do the following characters change into?

   i. Jupiter *Die Liebe der Danae*
   ii. Jupiter *Orphée aux Enfers*
   iii. Daphne *Daphne*
   iv. Acis *Acis and Galatea*

B. *The Rape of Lucrezia* has roots that go back not only to Shakespeare but beyond him to Ancient Rome. What Roman writer supplied the earliest inspirations?

C. Stephen Sondheim wrote music for a Greek drama "staged" in 1974 in the Yale Swimming Pool. What was it, and who was the original playwright?

12. SPARE PARTS

The following arias or ensembles start with a reference to specific areas of the human anatomy. Can you identify the operas they come from?

1. "Come to my Arms, my lovely Fair"
2. "Our arms intertwined"
3. "*O dolci Mani*" (hands)
4. "*Al tuoi piedi ci prostriamo*" (feet)
5. "Silvered is the raven hair"
6. "*En fermant les yeux*" (eyes)
7. "To pull-a da toot" (tooth)
8. "*In mia mano alfin tu sei*" (hand)
9. "*Sa main, sa douce main*" (hand)
10. "*Il me semble sur mon épaule*" (shoulder)
11. "Take a pair of sparkling eyes"
12. "*Sanft schloss schlaf dein Aug*" (eyes)
13. "*Placi d'alma, quieta il pietto*" (chest)
14. "*O grandi occhi*" (eyes)
15. "*Ferme tes yeux*" (eyes)

Extra Credit:

What are the fourteen areas of the body named in "A British tar is a soaring soul" from *H.M.S. Pinafore?*

13. CALL ME . . . IRRESPONSIBLE

Opera has given birth to some of the oddest names outside the novels of Dickens. Can you identify the works in which these characters appear?

1. Johnny Inkslinger
2. Lady Billows
3. Fireball Snedeker
4. Ko-Ko-Ri-Ko
5. Peep-Bo
6. Slender
7. Dr. Turtlespit
8. Little Bat

9. Snout
10. Mr. Splinters
11. Muff
12. Schlemiel
13. Peccadillo
14. General Boum
15. Pantaloon

Extra Credit:

A. What name did George Bernard Shaw use when he wrote his music criticisms?

B. Stephen Sondheim took another name for his authorship of lyrics to a song in *The Mad Show*. What was it?

C. In some operas, characters have descriptive titles rather than actual names. What operas do these groups of people appear in?

   I. The Secretary, the Foreign Woman, the Secret-Police Agent

   II. Hunchback, One-Eye, One-Arm

   III. The Music Master, the Composer, the Wig Master, the Dancing Master

   IV. The Princess, the Abbess, the Monitor

   V. The Captain, the Drum Major, the Doctor

14. RISING STARS

Can you match each singer at left to his or her professional debut role?

1. Dietrich Fischer-Dieskau
2. Monserrat Caballe
3. Gosta Winbergh
4. Leonie Rysanek
5. Franco Bonisolli
6. Eva Marton
7. José Carreras
8. Agnes Baltsa
9. Alfredo Kraus
10. Leontyne Price
11. Italo Tajo
12. Benita Valente
13. Jorma Hynninen
14. Johanna Meier
15. Nico Castel
16. Ileana Cotrubas
17. James Morris
18. Catherine Malfitano
19. Samuel Ramey
20. Marilyn Horne

a. Gennaro *Lucrezia Borgia*
b. Queen of Shemakha *Le Coq d'Or*
c. Hata *The Bartered Bride*
d. Fenton *Falstaff*
e. Mimi *La Bohème*
f. Crespel *Les Contes d'Hoffmann*
g. Zuniga *Carmen*
h. Rodrigo *Don Carlo*
i. Ruggero *La Rondine*
j. Mme. Lidoine *Dialogues of the Carmelites*
k. Agathe *Der Freischütz*
l. Nanetta *Falstaff*
m. Cherubino *Le Nozze di Figaro*
n. Duke of Mantua *Rigoletto*
o. Rodolfo *La Bohème*
p. Fafner *Das Rheingold*
q. Siebel *Faust*
r. Yniold *Pelléas et Mélisande*
s. Pamina *Die Zauberflöte*

Extra Credit:

A. Carlo Bergonzi had two professional debuts: as a baritone, and then, three years later, as a tenor. In what roles?

B. In what opera did Plácido Domingo make his professional debut as a conductor, and with what company?

C. What role was Frederica von Stade's professional debut in opera?

15. MODERN WORDS

Operas are usually referred to as works by such-and-such composer. Can you match the twentieth century works at left to their librettists?

1. *Of Mice and Men*	a. Horace Everett
2. *Peter Grimes*	b. Maurice Lena
3. *The Crucible*	c. T. Ricordi
4. *The Tender Land*	d. J.M. Synge
5. *Maria Golovin*	e. Giovacchino Forzano
6. *Dialogues of the Carmelites*	f. Montague Slater
	g. Gian Carlo Menotti
7. *Riders to the Sea*	h. Gertrude Stein
8. *Francesca da Rimini*	i. Sen Benelli
9. *L'Amore dei Tre Re*	j. Carlisle Floyd
10. *Le Jongleur de Notre-Dame*	k. Michael Tippett
	l. Bernard Stambler
11. *Il Tabarro*	m. Paul Schott
12. *Die Tote Stadt*	n. Giuseppe Adami
13. *Lodoletta*	o. Georges Bernanos
14. *King Priam*	
15. *The Mother of Us All*	

Extra Credit:

A. Novelist E.M. Forster was partly responsible for a libretto of a well-known Britten opera. What was it?

B. What famous composer had a hand in the libretto for Henze's *Elegy for Young Lovers*?

C. What composer is the librettist for Barber's *Vanessa*?

16. THE PERFECT WAGNERITE

Those of you who enjoy Wagner are blessed with the stamina to sit through *Die Meistersinger* (nearly six hours, counting intermissions) or a four-evening *Ring*. But how well did you pay attention during such events?

1. A total of how many tones and melodies does David's aria list as having to be mastered by a singer?

2. A minimum of how many faults will disqualify a singer from the competition?

3. In *Die Meistersinger*, who are, collectively, Christian, Peter, Niklaus, and Hans?

4. Which *Ring* character sings the line "*Wagalaweia! Wallala weiala weia*"?

5. Which *Ring* character sings the line "*Hehe! Hehe! Hieher! Hieher!*"

6. Which *Ring* character sings the line "*Ohe! Oh! au! Au!*"?

7. Which of Wagner's operas includes the refrain "*Hohohe! Johohe! Hoho! Ho! Ho!*"?

8. What is the name of the sword that Siegmund pulls from the ashtree?

9. About which goddess does the Shepherd in *Tannhäuser* sing?

10. Who sneezes while climbing about the rocks of the Rhine?

11. What mortal woman bears Alberich's child?

12. In a bit of Valkyrie humor, why should Ortlinde's and Helmwige's horses not be stabled together?

13. Who speaks the name of the yet-unborn Parsifal just before dying?

14. What kind of wind do the sailors in *Der Fliegende Holländer* consider lucky?

15. What is Siegfried's "Achilles' heel"?

Extra Credit:

Match the Meistersingers to their trades.

A. Hans Sachs	a. baker
B. Veit Pogner	b. town clerk
C. Kunz Vogelgesang	c. coppersmith
D. Konrad Nachtigall	d. goldsmith
E. Sixtus Beckmesser	e. soapboiler
F. Fritz Kothner	f. stocking maker
G. Balthasar Zorn	g. tinsmith
H. Ulrich Eisslinger	h. shoemaker
I. Augustin Moser	i. furrier
J. Hermann Ortel	j. pewterer
K. Hans Schwartz	k. tailor
L. Hans Foltz	l. grocer

17. STORMY WEATHER

Neither snow nor rain . . . makes the curtain go down on the following scenes. Can you identify the operas in which these take place?

1. A hurricane prevents a Great Work from being done.

2. Although she knocks at the door seeking shelter from the rain, the soprano knows that her entry means certain death.

3. A storm drives a hunter and huntress into each other's arms.

4. A doomed sailor is driven by storm into a Norwegian harbor.

5. Thunder rages as two enemies plan to settle a family feud with a duel.

6. An incestuous relationship gets its start during a rainstorm.

7. A tempest rocks the hero's boat as he sails home in triumph from battle.

8. Villagers become still more distrustful of the leading man when he sings a strange song during a squall.

9. A prince and his servant dry off at a peasant girl's house a few days after a ball which even she has attended.

10. A raging blizzard does not prevent a posse from pursuing their prey.

Extra Credit:

A. In what light opera, by a French composer better known for a serious grand opera, does a major character lose his sight during a storm?

B. In what opera by a famous German composer do two characters first meet on a ski slope?

C. In what Italian verismo opera does the heroine die in the snow outside her lover's house?

18. LAST WORKS

If you've had it up to here with all those child prodigies who
penned full-length operas in their cribs, let's see how good
you are at naming the LAST works (as determined by the
operas' premiere dates) by the following composers. Brown-
ie points if you can also remember who didn't live to finish
the job themselves.

 1. Verdi
 2. Puccini
 3. Bizet
 4. Offenbach
 5. Prokofiev
 6. Rossini
 7. Sullivan
 8. Bellini
 9. Wagner
10. Meyerbeer
11. Britten
12. Mozart
13. Tchaikovsky
14. R. Strauss
15. Rimsky-Korsakov

Extra Credit:

Donizetti produced three operas in his final year of opera
composition. What were they, and which was the very last to
premiere?

19. CROSSOVER QUIZ

Musicals have been wending their way into the classical world. Can you name the composer/lyricist teams responsible for the following works?

1. *Carousel*
2. *West Side Story*
3. *Porgy and Bess*
4. *Sweeney Todd*
5. *My Fair Lady*
6. *Kiss Me Kate*
7. *Show Boat*
8. *South Pacific*
9. *Candide*
10. *Kismet*
11. *Brigadoon*
12. *Song of Norway*
13. *The Pajama Game*
14. *The Sound of Music*
15. *A Little Night Music*

Extra Credit:

A. Who donated five million dollars—a million per year—to New York City Opera in exchange for the company's mounting of its 1986–1990 musical comedy spring season?

B. Which of the works listed above has been recorded by both the Scottish Opera and New York City Opera?

C. What member of the famed Algonquin Round Table contributed lyrics to the original *Candide*?

20. OK, WHO STARTED IT?

A dramatic device frequently used in opera is an ensemble in which all action stops as the principal characters tell the audience their feelings and thoughts (which they are still keeping private from each other). For each of the following, can you identify the character who begins the ensemble?

1. *Rigoletto* Act III Quartet
2. *Lucia di Lammermoor* Act II Sextet
3. *Les Contes d'Hoffmann* Venice Sextet
4. *Manon* Finale of Act IV
5. *Maria Stuarda* Act II concluding Sextet
6. *Faust* concluding Trio
7. *Il Barbiere di Siviglia* Final Trio
8. *La Traviata* Finale of Act II, Scene 2
9. *Die Zauberflöte* Finale
10. *Roméo et Juliette*, Finale Act III, Scene 2

Extra Credit:

Name the four singers of the *"Puritani* Quartet" and their roles.

21. WORLD OPERA

How well-traveled are you, musically-speaking?

1. What was the first opera presented at the Opéra Bastille when it opened in March 1990?

2. What Brazilian theater reopened for opera performance in 1990 after a hiatus of ninety-two years?

3. What opera company's *Ring* Cycle was inspired by the Washington, D.C., rapid-transit system?

4. What German opera house was destroyed by fire in November 1987—set by an arsonist who believed it was an office building?

5. In what city is there an annual Berlioz Festival?

6. In what country does the Ravenna Festival take place?

7. In what country does the Ravinia Festival take place?

8. *Satyagraha* was commissioned by the Arts Council of what city?

9. What opera, postponed for two years so that the tenor for whom the title role was written could star in it, had its world premiere in Barcelona in 1989?

10. What Austrian troupe made their U.S. debut in 1984 with a trio of lavish productions: *Die Fledermaus*, *Die Lustige Witwe*, and *Die Czárdásfürstin*?

11. What contemporary ensemble, founded by William Christie, specializes in producing baroque opera with period authenticity, its signature showpiece being Lully's *Atys*?

12. In 1988, Richard Bonynge discovered "lost" manuscript pages to what opera while going through ballet scores in the basement of the Royal Opera House at Covent Garden?

13. Torre del Lago hosts an annual festival in honor of what twentieth century composer?

14. What is the site of the annual festival that began in 1980 as one specializing in Rossinian works?

15. What opera was performed at Finland's Savonlinna Festival by the Central Opera of Peking in their first trip to the West in 1988—in Chinese?

Extra Credit:

A. Match these directors of the Bayreuth Festival with their terms of office. Note that, during one term, two people were co-directors.

I. Wolfgang Wagner	a. 1889–1908
II. Winifred Wagner	b. 1908–1930
III. Cosima Wagner	c. 1931–1944
IV. Wieland Wagner	d. 1951–1966
V. Siegfried Wagner	e. 1966 onward

B. What five opera productions did the Bolshoi Opera bring to the United States in their first tour to this country in 1975?

C. What four operas did the Teatro alla Scala bring to the U.S. in their first-ever tour to America in 1976?

22. FIRST THINGS FIRST

Into an article in *The Wall Street Journal*, a writer let slip the misnomer ANTONIO Rossini. Can you do better with the given names of these composers?

1. Leoncavallo
2. Ponchielli
3. Auber
4. Smetana
5. Zandonai
6. Giordano
7. Bellini
8. Glinka
9. Donizetti
10. Kálmán

Extra Credit:

A. What was Giacomo Meyerbeer's entire real name?

B. What was Fromental Halévy's entire real name?

C. What *was* Rossini's first name?

23. ECHOES

Some operas quote from other musical works. How adept are you at *déjà-entendu*?

1. In *The Ballad of Baby Doe*, whom does the cast in Act I Scene 1 go to listen to (though we never do get to hear her)?

2. In *Don Giovanni*, Mozart quotes from one of his own operas. What aria is it?

3. What is the original name of the Irish air heard in *Martha*?

4. What is used for Pinkerton's "American" leitmotif?

5. What opera is heard in rehearsal during *Captain Jinks of the Horse Marines*?

6. In *Le Donne Curiose*, Wolf-Ferrari quotes from a Venetian barcarole. What is its title?

7. *Orphée aux Enfers* quotes a line from what Gluck opera?

8. In *Les Contes d'Hoffmann*, what Mozart aria does Nicklausse mockingly sing a little of?

9. What Gilbert and Sullivan operetta is named in *The Pirates of Penzance*?

10. What Schumann song does Dr. P sing in *The Man Who Mistook His Wife for a Hat*?

Extra Credit:

A. In *Don Giovanni*, onstage musicians play music from operas by two composers other than Mozart. Whose, and what are the operas?

B What genuine school song is sung during *Street Scene*?

C. In what Offenbach operetta do young lovers who wish to marry plead their case with the girl's father in a pastiche bel canto trio sung in Italian doubletalk?

24. ROOTS

In the 7/27/86 issue of *The New York Times*, critic Donal Henahan put forth a case for the return of opera stories to their original locales, as opposed to updated settings. Can you recall the correct cities of the following plots?

1. *Così Fan Tutte*
2. *Die Lustige Witwe*
3. *I Puritani*
4. *Don Pasquale*
5. *Fidelio*
6. *Gianni Schicchi*
7. *Un Ballo in Maschera*
8. *Tosca*
9. *The Makropoulos Case*
10. *Le Villi*
11. *Don Giovanni*
12. *Arabella*
13. *Roméo et Juliette*
14. *Rigoletto*
15. *Lohengrin*

Extra Credit:

A. In what U.S. states do these take place:

    A. *Naughty Marietta*
    B. *Porgy and Bess*
    C. *Susanna*

25. AN OPERA BY ANY OTHER NAME

Many subtitles of well-known works have disappeared into obscurity—perhaps with just cause! Below, translated into English, are some examples of these. Can you name their "supertitles"?

1. Wedded Love
2. The Vain Precaution
3. The Market of Richmond
4. The Witch's Curse
5. The Triumph of Goodness
6. The Count of Essex
7. The Lass That Loved a Sailor
8. The King of Bataria
9. The Slave of Duty
10. The Two Peters

Extra Credit:

A. What opera is subtitled "The Two Windows"?

B. What opera is subtitled "The Inn of Terracine"?

C. *Les Troyens* is really a double-bill of two works. Name them.

26. FIRST SIGHTINGS

Can you name the city in which each of the following operas had its world premiere?

1. *The Love for Three Oranges*
2. *Werther*
3. *The Rake's Progress*
4. *I Vespri Siciliani*
5. *Suor Angelica*
6. *The Turn of the Screw*
7. *Lulu*
8. *Don Pasquale*
9. *Così Fan Tutte*
10. *La Forza del Destino*
11. *La Clemenza di Tito*
12. *L'Enfant et les Sortilèges*
13. *Dialogues of the Carmelites*
14. *The Gambler*
15. *I Puritani*

Extra Credit:

A. With what Verdi work did the Cairo Opera House open?

B. Where did the world premiere of *Amahl and the Night Visitors* take place?

C. Where did the first public opera house in the world open in 1637?

27. U.S. FESTIVALS

A valuable part of the American opera scene is its many music festivals, most of which take place during the summer.

1. What New York State summer arts community founded its own opera company in 1929?

2. Where did the PepsiCo Summerfare take place?

3. What avant-garde director enjoyed a close association with that festival?

4. Scottish composer Judith Weir's *A Night at the Chinese Opera* had its 1989 U.S. premiere in what opera company's summer season?

5. At what U.S. festival did the American premiere of Wagner's *Das Liebesverbot* take place in 1983?

6. Which U.S. festival has presented, as of summer 1989, a total of six world premieres and twenty-five American premieres, in addition to standard repertory?

7. At what New York City summer festival have such works as *La Finta Giardiniera, Idomeneo,* and *Acis und Galatea* been performed in concert form?

8. What U.S. music festival launched an all-American-cast *Ring* Cycle in 1985, believed to be the first of its kind?

9. In what city is Spoleto Festival USA based?

10. What opera has a special link with Central City Opera's summer season?

11. Why is *The Mighty Casey* a fitting feature of Glimmerglass Opera's repertoire?

12. In what U.S. state does Wolf Trap Opera perform?

13. For what festival was *Minutes Till Midnight* commissioned?

14. What opera company is based near New York's Glens Falls?

15. What opera company besides the Met has an annual summer season in New York City's Central Park?

Extra Credit:

A. Name the four Handel operas presented at Carnegie Hall's 1984–1985 Handel Festival in honor of the composer's 300th birthday year.

B. Name the four works in the opera-in-concert series presented by Carnegie Hall for its Centennial season, 1990–1991.

C. PepsiCo Summerfare concluded its existence in summer 1989 with three Mozart operas that had been performed there in past years—with much of the same casts. Name the operas that formed the 1989 program.

28. TWENTIETH CENTURY TRIPLETS

Below at left, twentieth century operas that are based upon plays, stories, or novels. Can you match the opera titles to their composers or original sources? Double your points bv linking up all three columns correctly.

A. *Sir John in Love*	1. Stravinsky	a. Melville
B. *Wuthering Heights*	2. Prokofiev	b. Benet
	3. Massenet	c. Shakespeare
	4. Shostakovich	d. Ouida
C. *Mavra*	5. Mascagni	e. Cervantes
D. *Betrothal in a Monastery*	6. Floyd	f. E. Bronte
	7. Vaughan Williams	g. Gogol
E. *The Devil and Daniel Webster*	8. Blitzstein	h. Sheridan
	9. Argento	i. Dickens
F. *Don Quichotte*	10. Moore	j. Pushkin
	11. Britten	k. H. James
G. *The Gambler*		l. Dostoyevsky
H. *Albert Herring*		m. Bunyan
I. *Billy Budd*		n. Hellman
J. *Regina*		o. de Maupassant
K. *The Pilgrim's Progress*		
L. *The Nose*		
M. *The Aspern Papers*		
N. *Lodoletta*		
O. *Miss Havisham's Fire*		

29. TELECASTS

Were you in front of the "idiot box" when these broadcasts aired?

1. Who sang the role of Madame Lidoine in the 1987 "Live from the Met" telecast of *Dialogues of the Carmelites*?

2. Who portrayed Pinkerton in New York City Opera's 1982 simulcast of *Madama Butterfly*?

3. Who directed the Met's 1978 telecast of *Tosca*, in his first season as staging director with that company?

4. What Monty Python player performed the role of Ko-Ko in the English National Opera production of *The Mikado* broadcast in North America in 1988?

5. What British-born tenor sang the role of Nanki-Poo?

6. Who sang the title role in the Opera Company of Philadelphia's televised *Faust*?

7. What 1977 New York City Opera simulcast placed television audiences in the dilemma of having to choose between watching the opera or the World Series?

8. Audio-recording sessions of what album featuring Tatiana Troyanos, Kiri Te Kanawa, and José Carreras were telecast in 1985?

9. PBS' seventeenth season of "Great Performances" in 1989 kicked off with a telecast of *Show Boat*. What company performed it?

10. Midway through their run of *Don Giovanni* during the Met's 1989–1990 season, basses Samuel Ramey and Ferruccio Furlanetto switched roles as the Don and Leporello. In the Salzburg production shown on U.S. television in 1988, which bass took which role?

11. Different telecasts in different years paired Beverly Sills and Plácido Domingo in special programs of music-related skits alongside a well-known actress-comedienne. Name her.

12. In 1984, PBS began showing a series of twelve Gilbert and Sullivan operettas cast with a combination of singers and actors. Who played Sir Despard Murgatroyd?

13. What tenor appeared as Don Ramiro in both the Ponnelle and Salzburg televised productions of *La Cenerentola*?

14. Who played the role when New York City Opera simulcast the work in the "Live from Lincoln Center" series?

15. In what year did the first televised "Pavarotti Plus!" concert take place?

Extra Credit:

A. Four artists in leading roles in the first "Live from the Met" telecast in 1977 appeared in another Met telecast of the same opera in 1982. Name the opera, the singers, and the roles they played.

B. The sets from five operas were used during the Met's two-part televised Centennial gala. Name the works the sets belonged to.

C. What five singers portrayed nineteenth century concert artists in the 1985 "Rossini in Versailles" broadcast?

30. SECRET LIVES

Below, some lesser-known facts about ten famous composers. Can you identify each man? For extra credit, answer the questions in parentheses.

1. Not only did he write many fairy-tale-based operas of his own, but he also created his own edition of a large-scale historical work written by a fellow countryman. (What was the opera?)

2. He wrote a nearly-forgotten opera based upon a play by Molière, as well as operas based on works of Goethe and Shakespeare. (What was the Molière-inspired work?)

3. He correctly predicted that a French opera—originally a flop—would become one of the world's favorites, and he was right. He wasn't, incidentally, a Frenchman. (What was the opera?)

4. Though most of his operas originated in his homeland, one of this composer's most popular works premiered in another country than his birth in a language of still another country. (What was the opera?)

5. As well as operas of his own, this composer wrote libretti for two other operas based on Shakespeare's plays. (Who composed those?)

6. This verismo composer hoped to write an opera based upon one of Shakespeare's great tragedies, but never realized his dream. (What play was this?)

7. He wrote the only opera believed to have ever had a continuous run of over 150 performances. (What was it?)

8. Better known for his operettas, this man performed in the orchestra pit of the Met when he first came to America. (What instrument did he play?)

9. This tenor, who sang the first German Calaf, also composed operettas. (With what composer is he most associated as a singer?)

10. Though he had wished to write operas drawn from the works of Poe, this French composer only created one such, unfinished work. (From which Poe story does it take this plot and title?)

31. PITCH PIPES

In place of castrati—now outlawed, to the relief of countless little boys of musical talent—modern-day opera productions offer another high vocal register rarity, countertenors. How much do you know about these roles and their singers?

1. What was the first opera produced at the Met, to employ countertenors in principal roles?

2. On what date was this historic event?

3. Who sang the two roles on that date?

4. What Britten opera calls for an other-worldly king to be sung by a countertenor?

5. What singer created the role?

6. Who performed the title role at the world premiere of *Akhnaten*?

7. What role in *Death in Venice* requires a countertenor?

8. Who created this role at its world premiere?

9. What Sondheim work, performed by some opera companies, calls for several leading female roles to be sung by men?

10. In *La Calisto*, what role is sung nowadays by a countertenor?

Extra Credit:

A. When the English National Opera produced *Xerxes* in 1988, how were the roles of Xerxes and Arsamene (originally sung by a castrato and a female soprano, respectively) cast?

B. What American countertenor has recorded an album of arias originally composed for the castrato Senesino?

C. What all-male troupe, which has performed internationally, sings standard female operatic roles in drag and in falsetto?

32. A MUSICAL MINORITY, PART I

Without including pre-twentieth century European operas such as *Otello* or *L'Africaine* (the latter of which is actually about a Hindu!), at first thought one might not know very much more about black singers, composers, lyricists, or settings of opera. However, the writer of this book easily collected enough material for at least three quizzes on the subject. Start here . . .

1. On whose novel was *Porgy and Bess* based?

2. Who was the first man to perform the role of Porgy?

3. Who was his first Bess?

4. In the 1959 film of the opera, what actor (dubbed by a singer) played Porgy?

5. In that film what actress, similarly dubbed by a singer, played Bess?

6. At the time of this printing, why must nearly every role in *Porgy and Bess* be performed by black artists?

7. What does Truman Capote's "The Muses Are Heard" have to do with this opera?

8. Who was the first black woman to sing a principal role at the Met?

9. What was it?

10. Who was the first black man to sing a principal role at the Met?

11. What was it?

12. Kurt Weill's *Street Scene* employed a black lyricist. Who?

13. In the list of roles in *Street Scene* is a black janitor who is given his own blues number. What is the man's name?

14. What internationally-renowned coloratura soprano appeared in the original Broadway cast of *West Side Story*?

15. What role did she play?

Extra Credit:

Name the professional debut roles of the following opera singers:

A. Willard White
B. Grace Bumbry
C. Jessye Norman
D. Leona Mitchell
E. Curtis Rayam
F. Barbara Hendricks

33. A MUSICAL MINORITY, PART II

1. What opera, which had its world premiere at New York City Opera, concerns a black slave accused of witchcraft?

2. What opera is based upon Alan Paton's *Cry, the Beloved Country*?

3. In what country is the opera set?

4. What Menotti opera is set in an African forest?

5. In what Verdi opera is a half-Incan character discriminated against and called a mulatto?

6. In what opera does a black Pullman porter become the emperor of an island in the West Indies?

7. Whose play is this work based on?

8. What white singer created the title role of this opera . . . in blackface?

9. Where was Scott Joplin born?

10. What is his only extant opera?

11. What is the origin of the character's title name, as explained in the course of the opera?

12. What do the conjurers in that work try to sell to people?

13. What Philip Glass opera features Martin Luther King as a leading figure?

14. What French opera, which premiered in 1856, features an aria sung by a slave on an American plantation?

15. To avoid political friction, a Brazilian opera originally about the liberation of African slaves was changed to concern Native Americans. What work is this?

Extra Credit:

A. What opera company produced the first North American staging of the opera of question 15, in 1989?

B. For whom did Gershwin compose the role of Porgy, but he turned it down?

C. What other Joplin opera existed long enough to be copyrighted, but has never been found?

34. A MUSICAL MINORITY, PART III

1. What Carlisle Floyd opera includes a quartet sung by black children celebrating the defeat of the Confederates?

2. In what state does the above opera take place?

3. What principal character of the above opera is revealed to be a member of the Ku Klux Klan?

4. What was the first American opera composed for an all-black cast?

5. Where is its action set?

6. What is the name of the quadroon slave in Victor Herbert's *Naughty Marietta*?

7. In *Show Boat*, what character is accused of being black and is thereby forbidden to act in shows on the work's vessel?

8. What British composer wrote an opera about Harriet Tubman?

9. What opera concerns the Haitian slaves' revolt against the French?

10. What black composer wrote it?

11. What is the name of the slaves' leader, a character based upon a genuine historical figure?

12. Who composed an opera about the life of Malcolm X?

13. Who wrote its libretto?

14. Who created its title role at the opera's world premiere?

15. What black soprano sang the role of Cleopatra in the Met's opening night performance in *Giulio Cesare*?

Extra Credit:

A. What nineteenth century tenor earned the nickname "the black Mario" (after Italian tenor Giovanni Mario)?

B. What soprano was dubbed "the black Patti" and went on to name her own opera troupe after that?

C. Who was the first black opera singer to appear in a white American opera company?

35. SHIPSHAPE

While opera usually takes place onstage, some operas take place on ships, or otherwise concern floating vessels.

1. Outside which town is the *H.M.S. Pinafore* anchored?

2. What must Idomeneo sacrifice to Neptune in return for being saved from a sea storm?

3. What is the name of Jake's boat in *Porgy and Bess*?

4. What enemy land is spotted by the crew during *Billy Budd*?

5. What body of water must William Tell cross to reach his home, in Act IV of Rossini's opera?

6. What Handel opera, performed at the Met, features an aria sung by a mermaid?

7. What is the name of the frigate that sinks in *Candide?*

8. In the "Boston" version of *Un Ballo in Maschera*, what is the name of the sailor who "gets lucky"?

9. In *Il Pirata*, Itulbo claims to be the captain of a ship from what foreign state?

10. What is the name of the brigantine in *La Gioconda?*

11. Where was Isabella headed, in *L'Italiana in Algeri*, when her boat was shipwrecked?

12. What is the name of the performance vessel in *Show Boat?*

13. In what bay does Daland's boat drop anchor as *Der Fliegende Holländer* opens?

14. What Gilbert and Sullivan character appears in both *H.M.S. Pinafore* and *Utopia Limited?*

15. In what opera does an aria *"Calo e mar"* ("Sky and sea") appear?

Extra Credit:

A. After what genuine ship was the original stage set of *H.M.S. Pinafore* modeled?

B. What was Gilbert's first choice for that operetta's name?

C. In *The Pirates of Penzance*, Ralph is praised for his skill at attacking vessels of what two companies?

36. MET OBSCURITY

While the Met stands for fame, it didn't help these operas very much. All were performed by that company less than ten times apiece. Can you name their better known composers?

1. *Il Matrimonio Segreto*
2. *Fra Diavolo*
3. *Saint Elizabeth*
4. *La Wally*
5. *Le Cid*
6. *Linda di Chamounix*
7. *Manru*
8. *Mireille*
9. *Nabucco*
10. *Prince Igor*
11. *L'Heure Espagnole*
12. *Dinorah*
13. *Il Signor Bruschino*
14. *La Campana Sommersa*
15. *Amelia Goes to the Ball*

Extra Credit:

A. What three operas were performed at the Met exactly once?

B. What opera, generally considered part of standard repertory, was—as of this printing—performed less than five times at the Met (back in 1916!)?

C. What opera, given at the met in 1891, was composed by Ernest II, the Duke of Saxe-Coburg?

37. PRIZE SONGS

In contrast to those losers of the last quiz, now let's have some winners!

1. In what year were the Metropolitan Opera Auditions established?

2. What two singers were the first winners?

3. Who was the first recipient of the Richard Tucker Award?

4. How much money did he win in that competition?

5. What do the following singers have in common with respect to a New York City-based singing competition?

   Shirley Verrett   Jan Opalach
   Dawn Upshaw   Barbara Hendricks

6. What was the first opera to win a Pulitzer Prize for music?

7. Who was the only composer to win two Pulitzer Prizes for operas?

8. What Douglas Moore opera won a Pulitzer Prize?

9. For what opera did Robert Ward win a Pulitzer Prize?

10. Who was the first singer to receive Musical America's "Musician of the Year" award?

Extra Credit:

A. What did the following pairs of artists have in common regarding a competition?

   Louis Quilico/William Lewis
   Martina Arroyo/Grace Bumbry
   Susan Dunn/Thomas Hampson

B. What opera composer won the first Pulitzer Prize for music, though not for an opera?

C. What Bizet opera was a winning submission in a contest sponsored by Offenbach?

38. WETTING THEIR WHISTLES

Not all operatic characters are teetotalers, as this list of beverages named onstage goes to show. Match each liquor to the opera in which it is mentioned.

1. *Wein der Sim*	a. *Der Rosenkavalier*
2. *Manzanilla*	b. *Arabella*
3. *Marsimino*	c. *Francesca da Rimini*
4. *Un bottaglia di Xeres*	d. *La Jolie Fille de Perth*
5. Tokay	e. *Vanessa*
6. *Un demigiana di Cipro*	f. *Don Giovanni*
7. *Du vieux whisky*	g. *Die Fledermaus*
d'Ecosse	h. *Der Fliegende Holländer*
8. *Montrachet*	i. *Lulu*
9. Elderberry wine	j. *Carmen*
10. *Vino di Scio*	k. *Falstaff*
11. *Romanee-Conti*	l. *Regina*
12. Moët-Chandor	
13. *Benediktiner*	
14. Madeira	
15. *Viel Sekt*	

Extra Credit:

A. In Offenbach's *Christopher Columbus*, what magic drink does the title character discover in America?

B. In what work do several characters compare the virtues of *xérès*, *malaga*, madeira, *alicante*, and port?

C. In what Offenbach operetta is a character dubbed Baron de Vermout von Bock-bier, Comte d'Avali-vintt-Katt-schopp-Vergiss Mein-nicht?

39. DIRECT THE DONS

Not a one a Donald, each "Don" on the left appears in a work named at right. Can you help them find their correct operas?

1. Don Antonio
2. Don Carlos
3. Don Fernando
4. Don Ramiro
5. Don Pedro
6. Don Marco
7. Don Cassandro
8. Don Diego
9. Don Andronico
10. Don Magnifico
11. Don Narciso
12. Don Ottavio
13. Don Alvaro
14. Don José
15. Don Alfonso

a. *Betrothal in a Monastery*
b. *La Finta Semplice*
c. *Béatrice et Bénédict*
d. *Don Giovanni*
e. *Il Turco in Italia*
f. *Fidelio*
g. *Così Fan Tutte*
h. *Ernani*
i. *Carmen*
j. *La Cenerentola*
k. *The Saint of Bleecker Street*
l. *La Forza del Destino*
m. *Il Guarany*
n. *Don Procopio*

Extra Credit:

A. What is another name for the Verdian character Ernani?

B. What Purcell opera is based upon the adventures of Don Juan?

C. In New York City Opera's roster during the 1960s through the 1980s, there was a man whose actual name was Don Carlo. What position did he have with the company?

40. BAG AND BAGGAGE

Even without having at their disposal the jets necessary for jet-setting, some opera composers sure got around! In what country was each of the following works actually composed?

1. Stravinsky's *Mavra*
2. Donizetti's *Don Pasquale*
3. Wagner's *Tristan und Isolde*
4. Spontini's *La Vestale*
5. Bellini's *I Puritani*
6. Mozart's *Mitridate, Re di Ponto*
7. Rossini's *Guillaume Tell*
8. Handel's *Orlando*
9. Stravinsky's *The Rake's Progress*
10. Wagner's *Der Fliegende Holländer*

Extra Credit:

A. In the context of this quiz, how was 1726 a momentous year for Handel?

B. Of what country did Stravinsky eventually become a citizen?

C. Of what country did Hindemith eventually become a citizen?

41. COUNTDOWN

Got your calculator ready? Match these ten operas to their composers.

1. *1000 Airplanes on the Roof*
2. *Nine Rivers from Jordan*
3. *The Seven Deadly Sins*
4. *Six Characters in Search of an Author*
5. *I Quattro Rusteghi*
6. *The Threepenny Opera*
7. *The Two Widows*
8. *Les Deux Aveugles*
9. *The Postman Always Rings Twice*
10. *Una Cosa Rara*

a. Paulus
b. Wolf-Ferrari
c. Martin y Soler
d. Smetana
e. Weisgall
f. Glass
g. Offenbach
h. Weill

Extra Credit:

A. In what Verdi opera is a man named Jacopo exiled by the Council of Ten?

B. What two composers created *Die Drei Pintos*?

C. How many operatic acts are in *Four Saints in Three Acts*?

42. EARLY AMERICAN OPERA

How much do you know about the "roots" of American opera? Take this quiz and find out.

1. What is considered the first American opera?

2. Who was the only composer to sign the Declaration of Independence?

3. What was the first foreign-language opera to be performed in its original language in North America?

4. What impressario was instrumental in presenting the American premieres of *Aïda*, *Carmen*, *Rigoletto*, and other works?

5. What was the first American opera based upon a native literary source?

6. What was the first grand opera composed in the United States?

7. During the first few decades of the nineteenth century, what city was considered the opera capital of the U.S.?

8. Under whose management did the "Swedish Nightingale," Jenny Lind, come to America?

9. Who is the first American composer to have had a work commissioned by the Met?

10. What was it?

Extra Credit:

A. Who was the first American-born woman to sing in a Wagnerian opera in the U.S.?

B. In what city did Minnie Hauk's operatic debut take place?

C. What was the first opera performed by the Juilliard School, in 1929?

43. TAKE A CHANCE

Opera often concerns gambling. What are your chances of answering the following?

1. What game do Tabor's cronies play during Act II of *The Ballad of Baby Doe*?

2. At what game does Guillot accuse the Chevalier des Grieux of cheating?

3. What card game is played in Act I of *La Fanciulla del West*?

4. Who is appointed banker in the above game?

5. With what hand does Minnie win her card game with Jack Rance?

6. What number do the dice players in *Porgy and Bess* want to come up?

7. When the ladies have their fortunes told in *Carmen*, how many cards does Frasquita have read?

8. Who tells Hermann the three cards that will win for him, in *Pique Dame*?

9. What game is in progress as the curtain comes up on *Fedora*?

10. When Robert le Diable has no more money with which to play at dice, what does he stake to continue playing?

11. Why does the Prince of Granada win the jousting tournament, without even jousting, in *Robert le Diable*?

12. What card game is played by Stroh and his cronies in *Intermezzo*?

13. At what game do people gamble in *La Gioconda*?

14. How much do Ferrando and Guglielmo bet that Dorabella and Fiordiligi will not be unfaithful to them?

15. At what German spa does Prokofiev's *The Gambler* take place?

Extra Credit:

A. In *Albert Herring*, Sid bets Albert double or nothing the price of his purchases at the greengrocer's. Had Albert accepted the bet and won, how much would Sid have had to pay up?

B. In what Italian opera are the words "Dooda, dooda, day"— from "Camptown Races"—sung onstage?

C. During the gambling match between the Chevalier des Grieux and Guillot, upon whom do Poussette and Javotte bet?

44. WE *ARE* AMUSED

Can you match each composer at left with a famous personage at right from whom he enjoyed special favor? (Several have more than one answer)

1. Cimarosa	a. Henry IV
2. Paisiello	b. Louis XIV
3. Spontini	c. Charles X
4. Cavalli	d. Catherine II
5. Lully	e. Queen Anne
6. Peri	f. Emperor Leopold II
7. Mozart	g. Napoleon
8. Handel	h. Louis XVIII
9. Rossini	i. Napoleon III
10. Auber	j. Emperor Joseph II

Extra Credit:

A. Haydn composed *L'Arianna Abbandonada* to showcase a soprano said to be the mistress of the Prince of Wales. Who was she?

B. When Beaumarchais's play *Le Barbier de Séville* was performed in a private production, the queen of France herself took the role of Rosina. Who was her husband?

C. What Gilbert and Sullivan operetta was given at Windsor for Queen Victoria?

45. A MUSICAL MENAGERIE

In spite of one or two predatory titles such as *Der Wildschütz* (The Poacher), opera boasts a number of works named for animals. Can you match these to their composers?

1. *The Bear*	a. Puccini
2. *Le Coq d'Or*	b. Mozart
3. *La Rondine*	c. Beeson
4. *L'Aiglon*	d. Floyd
5. *The English Cat*	e. Rossini
6. *L'Oca del Cairo*	f. Auber
7. *The Cunning Little Vixen*	g. Offenbach
	h. Britten
8. *Captain Jinks of the Horse Marines*	i. Walton
	j. Henze
9. *La Gazza Ladra*	k. Rimsky-Korsakov
10. *Le Docteur Ox*	l. Moore
11. *The White Horse Inn*	m. Janacek
12. *Albert Herring*	n. Benatzky
13. *The Wings of a Dove*	o. Honegger
14. *Of Mice and Men*	
15. *Le Cheval de Bronze*	

Extra Credit:

A. Which twentieth century composer, famous for his Fellini film scores, wrote an opera based on Hans Christian Andersen's *The Prince and the Swineherd*?

B. What French operetta about a dog was dubbed a . . . female dog . . . by the press?

C. What animal-inspired opera, given at the Met, also has an animal-name composer?

46. THE EASTERN SHUTTLE

Once outside the familiar boundaries of France, Italy, and
Germany, most operagoers' memories begin to go a little
blurry. Can you match these composers—all from Eastern
European countries—to their operas?

1. Bartók	a. *Kátya Kabanová*
2. Erkel	b. *Duke Bluebeard's Castle*
3. Dvořák	c. *Juliette*
4. Janáček	d. *Dalibor*
5. Kodaly	e. *Rusalka*
6. Smetana	f. *Halka*
7. Penderecki	g. *King Roger*
8. Martinů	h. *Háry János*
9. Szymanowski	i. *Hunyadi László*
10. Moniuszko	j. *The Devils of London*

Extra Credit:

A. *Duke Bluebeard's Castle* is said to have been influenced
by a Viennese work with which it has been performed as a
double-bill. Name the other opera.

B. Of the ten men above, which composer's last operatic
work is an unfinished adaptation of Shakespeare's *Twelfth
Night*, called *Viola*?

C. What Janáček opera is based upon Dostoyevsky's prison
diaries?

47. IN TECHNICOLOR

Moviegoers of the 1970s and 1980s won't have to leave their seats to answer these:

1. How many Academy Awards did *Amadeus* win?
2. Who conducted the score of the Zeffirelli movie *Otello?*
3. What Belgian bass-baritone starred in *The Music Teacher?*
4. Who conducted the Zeffirelli film *La Traviata?*
5. What Fellini movie concerns the funeral voyage of an opera star?
6. What film cast Klaus Kinski as a man obsessed with building an opera house in the Amazon?
7. Who played the throat therapist who fell for Pavarotti in *Yes, Giorgio?*
8. Who directed the 1984 film *Carmen* starring Domingo?
9. *Wagner,* starring Richard Burton, was originally a nine-hour British TV series. As a movie, how long does it run?
10. What movie, featuring Cher, contains several numbers from *La Bohème?*
11. What Vietnam film incorporates Wagner's "Ride of the Valkyries" into its score?
12. What Jack Nicolson movie contains *"Nessun dorma"* in its score?
13. What is the title of the documentary of Pavarotti's 1986 trip to China?
14. What opera is Dudley Moore shown conducting in the movie *Foul Play?*
15. The opera sets for the above scene belonged to another opera. Name it.

Extra Credit:

Name all ten directors of the multi-part film *Aria.*

48. VINTAGE OPERA FILMS

Were the questions in the last quiz a little too modern for you? Here's a quiz for old-movie buffs.

1. In what 1935 movie did Lawrence Tibbett play a struggling opera singer?

2. In what 1936 movie was Jeanette MacDonald's costar Clark Gable?

3. What was the first movie to pair up Jeanette MacDonald and Nelson Eddy?

4. Allan Jones and Mary Martin starred in what 1939 movie about an famous operetta composer?

5. In what 1948 movie did Jarmila Novotna play a mother looking for her lost son?

6. What 1938 movie about an operetta composer won an Oscar for Best Cinematography?

7. What soprano was showcased in that film?

8. In what 1952 movie did Mario Lanza play an opera singer who got drafted?

9. Kirsten Flagstad costarred with W.C. Field and Dorothy Lamour—among others—in what movie?

10. Deanna Durbin sang "Musetta's Waltz" and "*Ave Maria*" in what 1940 movie?

11. What Durbin film won an Oscar in 1937 for Best Musical Score?

12. What was unusual about Tito Gobbi's casting in the 1951 film of *Pagliacci*?

13. Lily Pons, Henry Fonda, and Lucille Ball appeared together in what 1935 film?

14. What 1930 movie includes a recital by John McCormack?

15. Who played the title role in the 1935 film *Mimi*, based on *La Bohème*?

Extra Credit:

The 1951 British film *Tales of Hoffman* (sic) was expertly dubbed by opera singers, its onscreen cast largely composed of actors and ballet dancers. Who supplied the voices for the following roles:

A. Lindorf
B. Nicklausse
C. Olympia
D. Giulietta
E. and F. And who both acted and sang two principal roles themselves?

49. KEEPING COUNT

Specific numbers come up in the course of many operas. How good are you at musical arithmetic?

1. Minnie asks Billy Jackrabbit to count to a certain number. What is it?

2. How long was Don José's prison sentence for letting Carmen escape?

3. How many years have Fiorilla and Don Geronio been married?

4. How many kisses does Tosca promise she will give Cavaradossi after his mock-execution is over?

5. At the start of *La Traviata*, how long has the Baron known Violetta?

6. How long has Alfredo secretly been in love with her?

7. How many years was the Dutchman's term at sea?

8. How many years had Augusta Tabor been married to Horace before she discovered his affair with Baby Doe?

9. How many years pass between the Prologue and Act I of *Simon Boccanegra*?

10. Ping mocks the deaths of Turandot's suitors, singing that one would be better off with a harem than with one Turandot. How many wives does he advocate that a man should take?

11. How long did Mandryka have the picture of Arabella before coming to woo her?

12. For how many years does Falstaff claim that he has helped Bardolf in food and drink, in Verdi's opera?

13. How many locks are on the chest stored in the Cave of Hercules in *Don Rodrigo*?

14. How many years of servitude does Kaspar still owe to Zamiel at the start of *Der Freischütz*?

15. What opera begins with two characters comparing notes on how many cars, planes, houses, and wives they have?

Extra Credit:

A. In what opera does an elderly mathematician sing a song about multiplication and the metric system?

B. According to the original stage directions, what number forms his hat?

C. What Gilbert and Sullivan character boasts about his expertise in calculus?

50. MUSICAL NOTES

Opera texts, not surprisingly, sometimes concern music.

1. In what opera are the composers Gluck, Lully, Rameau, Piccinni, and Couperin mentioned?

2. What two Richard Strauss operas are also name-dropped in the above work?

3. In what French opera are the French operas *Manon*, *Mignon*, and *Pré de Clerc* (sic) discussed?

4. What is the name of the onstage pianist in *Fedora*?

5. What operetta—about a fictional composer's need to supply a new waltz for a show—is based upon a motion picture released three years earlier?

6. In what opera does the main character exclaim at the sight of the work's genuine composer on a television screen?

7. In what opera is critic Andrew Porter mentioned?

8. In what non-French opera is a French song played on an offstage phonograph?

9. In the original production and traditional stagings of the above opera, whose voice is on the record?

10. Who is said to have been the composer of the song that the Marquise of Berkenfield wants Marie to sing?

11. In what opera does a character bemoan his contribution to the Spoleto Festival?

12. What is the name of the opera within Britten's *Let's Make an Opera*?

13. In what opera is there an amateur jazz ensemble of black performers who call themselves the Angel Band?

14. In what opera does a composer demonstrate the "electrododecaphonic" style of music?

15. What American opera concerns a composer who drowned in Lake Como?

Extra Credit:

A. In what Rossini opera are Haydn, Mozart, Beethoven, and Bach praised for their use of syncopation?

B. What is the name of the composer who is introduced to the guests at the Act I ball in *Andrea Chénier* along with the title character?

C. What is the name of the performance venue in *Zaza*?

51. IT'S ALL IN THE STARS

Though born in different years—yet sometimes appearing in the same "houses"—each twentieth century singer at left shares a birthday with another listed at right. Can you match the astral twins?

1. *Aries: 3/20-4/19*
   Franco Corelli—b. 4/8
2. *Taurus: 4/20-5/20*
   Birgit Nilsson—b. 5/17
3. *Gemini: 5/21-6/60*
   Beverly Sills—b. 5/26
4. *Cancer: 6/21-7/22*
   Nicolai Gedda—b. 7/11
5. *Leo: 7/23-8/22*
   Richard Fredricks—b. 8/15
6. *Virgo: 8/23-9/22*
   Arleen Augér—b. 9/13
7. *Libra: 9/23-10/22*
   Enzo Dara—b. 10/13
8. *Scorpio: 10/23-11/21*
   Joan Sutherland—b. 11/7
9. *Sagittarius: 11/22-12/20*
   Phyllis Curtin—b. 12/3
10. *Capricorn: 12/21-1/19*
    Sherrill Milnes—b. 1/10
11. *Aquarius: 1/20-2/18*
    Martina Arroyo—b. 2/2
12. *Pisces: 2/19-3/19*
    Christa Ludwig—b. 3/16

a. Teresa Stratas
b. Nicolai Ghiaurov
c. Gwyneth Jones
d. James Morris
e. Gabriel Bacquier
f. Maria Callas
g. Lisa Della Casa
h. Hermann Prey
i. Teresa Berganza
j. Rita Hunter
k. Walter Berry
l. Leona Mitchell

Extra Credit:

A. What two great tenors of the past had exactly the same birth dates?

B. What soprano and tenor were both born in the same year in Modena, Italy?

C. What pair of bass-baritone identical twins have swapped places onstage as the world's most look-alike Don Giovanni and Leporello?

52. OPERA IN GREAT BRITAIN

How much do you know about your English-speaking fellow opera-lovers across the sea?

1. What is London's largest opera house?

2. What is the former name of the English National Opera?

3. What distinguishes the troupe from the Royal Opera, with regard to audience comprehension of the operas' texts?

4. What annual summer festival is held in Sussex?

5. On whose estate is it held?

6. Who was the first artistic director of the Edinburgh Festival?

7. How many theaters in London have been called Covent Garden?

8. When was Covent Garden's resident opera company given the title "Royal Opera"?

9. What opera inaugerated the Royal English Opera House, now known as the Palace Theatre?

10. What is considered the first English opera?

11. What titled opera-lover founded *Opera* magazine in 1950?

12. What American conductor is the musical director of the Scottish Opera?

13. What national-level company is based in Leeds?

14. What national-level company is based in Cardiff?

15. What opera was performed in an arena—London's Earl's Court Exhibition Centre—in 1988?

Extra Credit:

A. Who founded the Aldeburgh festival, and why is it held at that site?

B. What briefly-existent opera troupe, organized by and named for a famous conductor, produced Russian operas using sets left behind when the Diaghilev Company fled England at the start of World War I?

C. On what English politician do historians believe the character of Macheath in *The Beggar's Opera* was based?

53. THE INN SPOTS

Each of the restaurants, inns, hotels, and taverns at left features in an opera at right. Can you match them up?

1. Windsor Hotel	a. *Andrea Chénier*
2. Boar	b. *La Rondine*
3. The Golden Lily	c. *La Périchole*
4. Grundslee Inn	d. *La Fanciulla del West*
5. Tiro	e. Auber's *Manon Lescaut*
6. Polka	f. *Intermezzo*
7. Clarendon Hotel	g. *Peter Grimes*
8. Willard Hotel	h. *Werther*
9. Café Hottot	i. *The Ballad of Baby Doe*
10. The Three Cousins	j. *Fedora*
11. Palmetto	k. *Falstaff*
12. The Blue Dial	
13. The Golden Grape	
14. Bancelin's	
15. Garter Inn	

Extra Credit:

A. What five establishments are recommended as places that Ruggero should visit, in *La Rondine*?

B. In what opera does an unnamed inn bear a sign that translates to "Good lodging for good money"?

C. In what inn hangs a sign with the motto "*Honny soit qui mal y pense*"?

54. COLD CASH

If you think ticket prices are high, look at the kind of money that changes hands during opera performances!

1. What bribe does Cavaradossi promise the jailor in return for delivering a letter to Tosca?

2. How much does Pinkerton owe Goro for Butterfly?

3. What amount does Gianni Schicchi allow for funeral expenses?

4. How much has the painting of Lulu as a dancer sold for?

5. How much does Nemorino pay for his love philtre?

6. How much does Porgy give Frazier for Bess's "divorce" from Crown?

7. What does Billy Jackrabbit pay Wowkle's father in order to marry her?

8. How much does Don Giovanni pay Leporello to swap places with him?

9. What is Abdul's payment for pretending to be a caveman, in *The Last Savage*?

10. What bill does Norina ring up while buying hats after her "marriage" to Don Pasquale?

11. How much does the Chevalier des Grieux inherit from his mother?

12. What does Ochs demand as compensation besides his dowry?

13. What is Basilio's payment for witnessing Almaviva's marriage to Rosina?

14. What is the opera troupe's payment for performing "Ariadne" in *Ariadne auf Naxos*?

15. Who proposes to present a bill to Parliament levying a tax on fat people?

Extra Credit:

A. Who shows off a framed dollar—the first he earned—to his daughter's suitor?

B. In what opera do the characters take up a collection for a man's funeral by dropping money into a saucer on the deceased man's chest?

C. Who composed the operetta *Die Dollarprinzessin*?

55. BOOKWORMS

Some operatic characters display their cultural depth by making references to literary works or legends. Match the names at left to the operas in which they are mentioned.

1. Tristan and Isolde
2. Otello and Iago
3. Don Juan and Elvira
4. Roxane
5. El Cid
6. Prince Charming and Sleeping Beauty
7. The Fox (and the Grapes)
8. Pandora
9. Orlando Furioso
10. Lancelot (Galeotto) and Guenevere

a. *Fedora*
b. *Capriccio*
c. *Don Quichotte*
d. *L'Elisir d'Amore*
e. *Manon Lescaut*
f. *Chérubin*
g. *Francesca da Ramini*
h. *Louise*
i. *La Serva Padrona*

Extra Credit:

A. In what opera are Hamlet's soliloquy, Hermione's death, and Bossuet's funeral oration all clumped together as examples of "classics"?

B. In what German opera is Pascal quoted?

C. Blake and Wilde are quoted in what American opera?

56. SONGFEST

Each of the songs at left does not appear in any opera, but—often sung in soloist recitals—was penned by an opera composer at right. Match them up.

1. *"Les filles de Cadix"*
2. *"Ouvre tes yeux bleux"*
3. *"Clair de lune"*
4. "Suleika"
5. *"Er ist's"*
6. *"Le spectre de la rose"*
7. *"La flute enchantée"*
8. *"Ballade des gros dindons"*
9. "None But the Lonely Heart"
10. *"La danza"*
11. *"Warnung"*
12. *"Chanson d'avril"*
13. "The Last Chord"
14. *"Zueignung"*
15. *"Si mes vers avaient des ailes!"*

a. Hahn
b. Bizet
c. Strauss
d. Tchaikovsky
e. Debussy
f. Ravel
g. Rossini
h. Schubert
i. Mozart
j. Berlioz
k. Sullivan
l. Chabrier
m. Schumann
n. Délibes
o. Massenet

Extra Credit:

What twentieth century composers wrote the following song cycles?

A. "Knoxville, Summer of 1915"
B. "The Holy Sonnets of John Donne"
C. "Songfest"

57. SILVER NOTES AMONG THE GOLD

These opera composers all lived past eighty. How old were they on their final birthdays?

1. Camille Saint-Saëns
2. Ralph Vaughan Williams
3. Gustav Charpentier
4. Pietro Mascagni
5. Luigi Cherubini
6. Virgil Thomson
7. Richard Strauss
8. Giuseppe Verdi
9. Igor Stravinsky
10. Darius Milhaud

Extra Credit:

A. At what age did tenor Hugues Cuénod make his Met debut?

B. What opera, by then-eighty-four-year-old Sir Michael Tippett, had its world premiere at the Houston Grand Opera in 1989?

C. What conductor led his first *Ring*, with the Seattle Opera, at the age of eighty-two?

58. HIGH FASHION

Costume of course bears a great deal of importance in opera. How fashion conscious are you?

1. For whom does Porgy buy a hat trimmed with feathers?

2. In what opera does Act II begin with the heroine applying cosmetics and two decorative patches?

3. To what article of clothing does the ribbon that Cherubino steals belong?

4. What is the name of the Marschallin's hairdresser?

5. Who sings an aria called "*Quella del velo*"—a song about a veil?

6. How does Emilia obtain Desdemona's handkerchief in Verdi's *Otello*?

7. In what opera is the dropping of a royal crown taken as a terrifying omen?

8. Who goes skinnydipping in that opera?

9. In what opera do seamstresses discuss how to bone and pad the clothes on which they are working?

10. In what opera does an English tailor veto sewing a zipper into a pair of trousers?

11. Who becomes angry when her father tells her to sew a plain gown for herself, because her stepmother has just bought a new, expensive dress?

12. Where does Fedora hide and carry a fatal dose of poison?

13. In what opera does a woman, envious of another's gown, demand that her party guests dance a fast dance that will make them perspire, so that when the ladies retire to change into dry clothing, she may swipe the dress and put it on herself?

14. What does Dulcinée ask Don Quichotte to retrieve from a bandit, in Massenet's opera?

15. What opera features a cosmetics-peddler called Lazuli?

Extra Credit:

A. As has been documented in several autobiographies, Beverly Sills once cut up a costume rather than wear it, because she felt its color didn't suit her. What opera was this connected with?

B. During the 10/24/87 New York City Opera performance of *Tosca*, the soprano playing the title role caught her heavy gown on a staircase and had to sing part of Act I tethered to the scenery until a member of the company had the presence of mind to come forth and cut her free. Who was the unfortunate diva?

C. In recent years, the Met production of a certain opera has required that its orchestra and conductor wear casual clothing during the first half of the work, and then change into formal evening dress for the remainder of the show. What opera is it?

59. WHAT'S IN A NAME

How keenly have you listened to the name-dropping that occurs in opera?

1. In what opera are the names "Sorenson," "Seligman," and "Sokoloff" heard?

2. Who are Madelon, Ninetta, Caton, Regina, Claretta, Violetta, Nerina, Ninon, and Georgetta, as a group?

3. What name did Dr. Schön give to Lulu?

4. What did Dr. Goll call her?

5. What is the name of the Italian tenor in *Capriccio*?

6. What is the name of Louise's father?

7. Whose second through sixth names are Maria Ehrenreich Bonaventura Ferdinand Hyacinth?

8. What is the Marschallin's nickname for Octavian?

9. What was Augusta Tabor's maiden name?

10. What is Captain Vere's full name?

11. By what name is Henry of Ofterdingen better known?

12. By what name does Louisa Miller's noble suitor call himself when he is disguised as a peasant?

13. What is the name of the maiden from whom Desdemona learned the "Willow Song"?

14. By what false names does Miss Pinkerton in *The Old Maid and the Thief* tell Bob to call himself?

15. Who is the bearer of the marriage contract of Don Pasquale and "Sofronia"?

Extra Credit:

A. Name Mandryka's three servants.

B. By what names are Ferrando and Guglielmo listed on the false marriage contract?

C. What four servants are called in to help toss Falstaff out the window, when he is hidden in the laundry basket in Verdi's opera?

60. MARK YOUR CALENDARS

Can you supply the specific dates (degree of detail sometimes indicated in parentheses) to these items?

1. On what date (month/day/year) is Albert Herring chosen as King of the May?

2. What date (month/day/year) does the final scene in *X* depict?

3. What is the date (month/day/year) that the will is drawn up in *Gianni Schicchi*?

4. What is Frederic's birthday (month/day) in *The Pirates of Penzance*?

5. In what year will he turn twenty-one, by the pirates' reckoning?

6. In what year did Captain Vere command his ship, as described in *Billy Budd*?

7. In what year does *Arabella* take place?

8. On what date (month/day/year) does *Casanova* open?

9. In what month and year does Horace Tabor have his hallucinatory last scene in *The Ballad of Baby Doe*?

10. In what month and year does Act II of *Andrea Chénier* take place?

11. In what year is *La Muette de Portici* set?

12. On what date (month/day/year) does the investigation that occurs in *Miss Havisham's Fire* take place?

13. In what year is *La Juive* set?

14. In what year does Verdi's *Attila* take place?

15. In what year does *Regina* take place?

Extra Credit:

A. During what Chinese year were twelve suitors' heads chopped off in *Turandot*?

B. On what date (month/day/year) did Lady Billows's father shoot the otter whose pelt since became her purse?

C. What is the complete title of the operetta more commonly known as *Monsieur Choufleuri*?

61. SKIRTING THE ISSUE

"Pants roles"—women dressing up as men—are common to opera. More rarely does the reverse occur.

1. What name does Octavian take when disguised as a woman?

2. What names does le Comte Ory take when he dresses as a nun?

3. In *Daphne*, who disguises himself as a woman in order to win the affection of the title character in a sisterly fashion?

4. In what Poulenc opera do a husband and wife exchange sexual roles?

5. How many children does the husband bear?

6. In *Mavra*, the title role is taken by what male character who is pretending to be a female cook?

7. How is he found out?

8. In what Donizetti one-act opera is a pushy stage mother played by a baritone?

9. In Act III of *Le Nozze di Figaro*, who is the one to reveal that the befrocked Cherubino is really a boy?

10. In what twentieth century opera is there an opera-within-an-opera featuring a performer who is supposedly a castrato playing a woman—and the singer turns out to really be a woman?

11. In what Offenbach operetta are the women of the title portrayed by men?

12. In *Candide*, which male character is proposed to by a man while disguised as a woman?

13. In *The Love for Three Oranges*, what female role is sung by a bass?

14. In *Falstaff*, who dresses up to take Nanetta's place as Queen of the Fairies?

15. In *A Midsummer Night's Dream*, which of the rustic players performs the female role of Thisbe in their play?

Extra Credit:

A. In what modern American opera does a bisexual Russian prince perform a cabaret scene partially in drag?

B. In Act IV of *La Bohème*, when the four roommates dance together, who momentarily acts the part of a shy young maiden?

C. In Cavalli's *La Calisto*, which female role is played throughout by a man?

62. ANIMAL HOUSE

As anyone in theatrical circles knows, life backstage can sometimes resemble a zoo. Onstage . . . as well!

1. What animal does Don Magnifico dream about?

2. What animal is featured on Otello's emblem?

3. Whose menagerie includes a tiger, a bear, and a crocodile?

4. In what opera is an old dog taken away to be shot?

5. In what opera are lapdogs and parrots offered for sale?

6. What animal draws the traveling theater cart in *Pagliacci*?

7. What is the name of Mrs. Jones's dog in *Street Scene*?

8. Who says that animals never cheat on each other, but men are unfaithful?

9. In what opera does the leading tenor brag about how he killed a bear?

10. In what opera does the title character turn out to be an ape?

11. What turn-of-the-century composer, more famous for longer operettas, wrote a short work called *The Zoo*?

12. Edgardo rescued Lucia from an attack by what animal?

13. What is the name of Smithy's frog, in *The Jumping Frog of Calaveras County*?

14. How does a gambler attempt to "fix" the frog-jumping match?

15. In what crossover work does an ensemble include the voices of two sheep and a lion?

Extra Credit:

A. In what Britten opera are there two singing cats and a singing dog?

B. In what Britten opera does a chorus sing about a cow jumping over the moon?

C. In *Der Freischütz*, what is the name of the dog Annchen's aunt once mistook for a ghost?

63. APPETIZERS

What do these fifteen works have in common?

1. *Ariadne auf Naxos*
2. *La Bohème*
3. *Otello*
4. *Elektra*
5. *Die Frau ohne Schatten*
6. *Susannah*
7. *Tosca*
8. *L'Amore dei Tre Re*
9. *La Serva Padrona*
10. *Pelléas et Mélisande*
11. *Salome*
12. *Wozzeck*
13. *Noye's Fludde*
14. *Oedipus Rex*
15. *Vanessa*

Extra Credit:

A. The overture to *Elisabetta, Regina d'Inghilterra* was first used for what other historical opera?

B. Which operatic overture would Mahler sometimes shift to introduce Act II instead of Act I when he conducted this opera, so that latecomers wouldn't miss it?

C. For which of his works did Verdi compose, but then decide not to use, a new overture forty-six years after the opera's premiere?

64. SAINTS ALIVE!

Match the saints at the left to the operas in which they are mentioned or exist as a character. This is a tricky one: some saints appear in more than one opera, some operas have more than one saint, and some saints share names.

1. Michael
2. John
3. Rosalie
4. Genevieve
5. Augustine
6. Ignatius Loyola
7. Margaret
8. Valentine
9. Just
10. Giles
11. Louis
12. Crispin
13. T(h)eresa
14. Peter
15. Agnes

a. *La Jolie Fille de Perth*
b. *Don Carlo*
c. *Mireille*
d. *Four Saints in Three Acts*
e. *Der Mond*
f. *Robert le Diable*
g. *Die Meistersinger von Nürnberg*
h. *Grisélidis*
i. *La Vie Parisienne*
j. *Manon*
k. *Jeanne d'Arc au Bucher*
l. *The Rake's Progress*
m. *Il Viaggio a Reims*

Extra Credit:

A. In what opera do several ladies run through a number of saints' names while trying to guess the name of a shy young stranger?

B. In what opera is there a character called St. Settlement?

C. In the Mini-Met production of the traditionally all-black
Four Saints in Three Acts, what tenor was the only white
principal artist in the cast?

65. FATHER TIME

Certain events in opera take place at specific times. Can you
give the hours when the following take place?

1. Don Carlo declares his love to Eboli, thinking she is
   Elisabetta.
2. Violetta awakens in her bedroom.
3. Curtain time for the play in *Pagliacci*.
4. When Nedda plans to meet Silvio.
5. Falstaff's appointed hour at the Oak of Herne.
6. The end of Act I of *Louise*.
7. The beginning of Act II of *Louise*.
8. Sid's planned date with Nancy, in *Albert Herring*.
9. The peddlers in *Lakmé* pack up and leave the marketplace.
10. When Golaud's horse took fright and threw him.
11. Golaud warns Pelléas to avoid Mélisande.
12. Dr. Malatesta's expected arrival.
13. When Olivier wishes to meet Madeleine.
14. Ourrias's boat sinks.
15. The portrait of Cuno fell and struck Agathe.

Extra Credit:

A. In *L'Heure Espagnole*, which two characters are hidden
inside grandfather clocks?

B. From what time of morning to what time of night will
Phoebe stay by Fairfax's side, or so she swears in *The
Yeomen of the Guard*?

C. In *Falstaff*, during what period of day is Ford absent from
home?

66. SPECIAL MENTION

Each person on the left never appears in the opera in which he or she is mentioned, yet each is the subject of a song within a work listed at right. Can you pair up the person to the operatic source? Note: one lucky lady is sung about in two operas.

1. Piquillo	a. *La Wally*
2. Fatima	b. *Don Pasquale*
3. Vilia	c. *Roberto Deveraux*
4. Joe	d. *Monsieur Choufleuri*
5. Nerina	e. *La Périchole*
6. Riccardo	f. *Sappho*
7. Rosamunda	g. *Die Lustige Witwe*
8. Queen Mab	h. *Les Contes d'Hoffmann*
9. Robin	i. *Mireille*
10. Rosalinde	j. *La Traviata*
11. Kleinzach	k. *Peter Grimes*
12. Max de Sedlitz-	l. *Roméo et Juliette*
Calembourg	m. *Manon*
13. Doretta	n. *Le Jongleur de Notre-*
14. Pedro	*Dame*
15. Magali	o. *La Rondine*
	p. *La Grande Duchesse de*
	Gérolstein

Extra Credit:

A. During what aria does the Duke of Mantua refer to himself as Gualtier?

B. In *Porgy and Bess*, who sings a song about "Ole Man Sorrow"?

C. In what opera is there a ragtime number about a woman called Aunt Dinah?

67. AN OPERATIC AVIARY

"Canary parts" aside, opera does contain a number of references to our feathered friends. How attentive were you to their species?

1. What bird does Max shoot in Act I of *Der Freischütz*?

2. What bird does Agathe dream about?

3. What bird do Susannah and her brother sing about, in *Susanna*?

4. In what Britten opera do the characters include a dove and a raven?

5. What bird is the subject of Antonia's first aria in *Les Contes d'Hoffmann*?

6. In what Offenbach operetta does a dove fly down from Mount Olympus with a message?

7. In what Gilbert and Sullivan operetta is the subject of an Aesop fable—a jackdaw in peacock's feathers—listed along with other ominous proverbial allusions?

8. In what opera does a character sing about a turtledove in a vulture's nest?

9. In *La Bohème*, what bird is said to have met its death from consuming parsley?

10. Which of her birds does Baba the Turk love best?

11. What birds fly out of the tower as Pelléas strokes Mélisande's hair?

12. In what crossover work is a bird's neck broken onstage?

13. What is the name of Richard's ship, in *Ruddigore*?

14. Who gave King Dodon the Golden Cockerel?

15. In what Gilbert and Sullivan operetta is there a song about a cock who doesn't crow?

Extra Credit:

A. In what opera, otherwise performed in English, does a character sing about "*l'hirondelle*," "*la rossignol*," and "*le corbeau*"?

B. In what opera do seven varieties of birds sing in a garden at midday?

C. In what opera does a fox incite chickens to revolt against a rooster?

68. OUCH!

Along with "indisposed" performers, opera has its fill of ailing characters.

1. What injury causes Baron Ochs to literally scream murder?

2. What treatment does Figaro demand from Dr. Bartolo, during the shaving scene in Rossini's opera?

3. Who sneezes several times during *L'Italiana in Algeri*?

4. What bel canto work contains a trio in which one character sneezes while another can't stop yawning?

5. In what opera do choristers and the leading tenor feign laryngitis in order to go on strike for better conditions at the theater at which they are engaged to sing?

6. What operetta includes an aria dubbed "The Migraine Song"?

7. In what operetta does the title character sing "The Seasick Song"?

8. What disease afflicts the city in *Death in Venice*?

9. What operatic character has been recovering from fractured ribs?

10. Who sings that he will row his boat despite being blistered on both his hand and his backside?

11. What disease does Lulu catch while in prison?

12. In *Sweeney Todd*, who sells a miracle elixir?

13. In a sometimes-cut aria in *Candide*, it is inferred that a certain disease caused Pangloss to require an artificial nose. What is it?

14. What poison do Ferrando and Guglielmo pretend to take?

15. Why does Susanna decline to keep the Countess's smelling salts for herself?

Extra Credit:

A. In the Peter Sellars staging of *Così Fan Tutte*, what celebrity does Despina pretend to be when she comes forth to "cure" Ferrando and Guglielmo?

B. What kind of doctor does Almaviva, disguised as a soldier, claim to be?

C. In what opera is a woodchopper passed off as a doctor?

69. FIRST PERSON

The opera personalities at left—sometimes with a little help from others—all have written books about themselves or their stage-related ideas. Can you match the writers to their works, listed at right?

1. Hermann Prey	a. *5,000 Nights at the*
2. Renata Scotto	*Opera*
3. Plácido Domingo	b. *Musical Chairs*
4. Sir Rudolf Bing	c. *My Road to Opera*
5. Elisabeth Söderstrom	d. *Subsequent*
6. Jonathan Miller	*Performances*
7. Robert Merrill	e. *My First 40 Years*
8. Boris Goldovsky	f. *Findings*
9. Schuyler Chapin	g. *A Knight at the Opera*
10. Leonard Bernstein	h. *My Life in Pictures*
11. Birgit Nilsson	i. *More Than a Diva*
12. Frank Corsaro	j. *Between Acts*
13. Dietrich Fischer-Dieskau	k. *Reverberations*
14. Marian Anderson	l. *My Lord, What a*
15. Harold Prince	*Morning*
	m. *First Night Fever*
	n. *Contradictions*
	o. *Maverick*
	p. *In My Own Key*

Extra Credit:

A. What then-member of the Metropolitan Opera House staff wrote *The Authentic Pasta Cookbook*, published in 1985?

B. What American bass has collected interviews with colleagues into a volume called *Great Singers on Great Singing*?

C. What are the titles of Beverly Sills's three published autobiographies?

70. STRANGER THAN TRUTH

There are also fictional accounts of the world of opera—
several written by singers themselves. Can you match these
books to their correct authors?

1. *Elegy for a Soprano*
2. *Diva*
3. *Prima Donna at Large*
4. *Cry to Heaven*
5. *The Hamster Opera Company*
6. *Gala*
7. *A Cadenza for Caruso*
8. *O Paradiso!*
9. *Murder at the Opera*
10. *The Divas*

a. Barbara Paul
b. William Lewis
c. Delacorta
d. Robert Merrill (w/Fred Jarvis)
e. (editor) Thomas Godfrey
f. Anne Rice
g. Janis Mitchell
h. Kay Nolte Smith
i. Conrad L. Osborne

Extra Credit:

A. In 1970, a novel called *Philharmonic* was based, by co-authors Herbert Russcol and Margalit Banai, on the life of a well-known composer-conductor. Name him.

B. In the late 1980s, four hardback comic-book style English translations of libretti were published in association with the Royal Opera House at Covent Garden. Of what four operas did they tell the stories?

C. The story concerned the creation of a Wagnerian-like opera called *The Giant*. The author was a famous mystery writer breaking away from her genre work under the pseudonym of Mary Westmacott. Give the title and author of the book.

71. IT'S A LIVING

Can you match each operatic character at left with his or her trade?

1. Dr. Kolenaty *The Makropoulos Case*
2. Guccio *Gianni Schicchi*
3. Sellem *The Rake's Progress*
4. Irene Giroux *Postcard from Morocco*
5. Rabonnier *La Rondine*
6. Paolino *Il Matrimonio Segreto*
7. Cal *Regina*
8. Mr. Gedge *Albert Herring*
9. Assan *The Consul*
10. Euthycles *La Belle Hélène*
11. Quince *A Midsummer's Night's Dream*
12. M. Javelinot *Dialogues of the Carmelites*
13. Creonte *The Love for Three Oranges*
14. Frick *La Vie Parisienne*
15. M. Taupe *Capriccio*

a. glass-cutter
b. blacksmith
c. cook
d. lawyer
e. prompter
f. butler
g. doctor
h. bootmaker
i. dyer
j. hatmaker
k. vicar
l. painter
m. auctioneer
n. bookkeeper
o. carpenter

Extra Credit:

A. In what opera does a photographer put forth that laborers want to be tradesmen; tradesmen, lords; lords, artists; and artists, gods?

B. In what Offenbach work does a character describe, in an aria, an interview he has had at an employment agency where he has gone to seek a housekeeper?

C. What opera cast includes two journalists, four Spanish dancers, a waiter, a butler, and a fireman?

72. THE MODERN AGE

While we tend to associate opera with period settings, we forget that our own time has its own distinctive images and objects that have made their way into musical works.

1. What electrical appliance is an important element of *La Voix Humaine*, *The Consul*, and *Trouble in Tahiti*?

2. In what Poulenc opera is there a reference to ration cards?

3. What opera concerns the efforts of steelworkers to form a union?

4. In Jonathan Miller's controversial "Little Italy" *Rigoletto* staging, what "accompanies" the Duke as he sings "*La donna è mobile*"?

5. In what opera does a woman singing a lullaby to her grandchild promise the baby, among other things, planes?

6. In what Britten opera is a buzz-saw mentioned?

7. What Prokofiev opera concerns a Soviet pilot?

8. In what opera does a soprano sing to music issuing from a tape recorder?

9. In what opera does a saint pose for a photograph?

10. What short Douglas Moore opera takes place on the set of a hospital-type TV soap opera—complete with commercial breaks?

Extra Credit:

A. In what opera is Einstein depicted?

B. In what operetta is a character called Microscope?

C. What is the name of the movie Dinah describes in *Trouble in Tahiti*?

73. OPERA U.S.A.

America's many opera companies besides the Met have made important contributions to the art. How well do you know what has been happening around the country?

1. At what opera company did Leonard Bernstein's *A Quiet Place* have its world premiere in 1983?

2. What former singer assumed the role of general manager of the Lyric Opera of Chicago in 1981?

3. What was the first U.S. company to perform all three of the composer's only complete operas in a special Monteverdi cycle in 1988?

4. What editor/critic/commentator succeeded founder Glyn Ross as general director of the Seattle Opera in 1983?

5. What Canadian bass-baritone took over management of the Washington Opera in 1975?

6. With what opera was Houston Grand Opera's Wortham Center inaugurated in 1987?

7. The Luciano Pavarotti International Voice Competition is associated with what U.S. opera company?

8. Who directed the 1985 San Francisco Opera *Ring* cycle?

9. Who founded San Francisco's Pocket Opera in 1968?

10. What was the first opera presented, in the work's world premiere, by the Opera Center of Washington, in the John F. Kennedy Center Opera House when the center opened in 1971?

11. *Summer and Smoke* premiered at what opera company?

12. Where did the U.S. premiere of *Akhnaten* take place?

13. In 1984, the Dallas Opera acquired an intimate performing space called the Majestic Theatre. What had the building been used for until then?

14. Who directed the Seattle Opera *Ring* cycle in 1986?

15. What opera company gave Verdi's *Il Corsaro* its first complete U.S. staging in 1982?

Extra Credit:

A. Two different operas based upon Henry James's *The Aspern Papers* coincidentally had their world premiere on the same date: 11/19/88. Where did the performances take place?

B. With what company did P.D.Q. Bach's *The Abduction of Figaro* have its world premiere?

C. When the San Francisco earthquake of 10/17/89 hit the city, what San Francisco Opera performance due to go on that night had to be called off?

74. MUCKY-MUCKS

Can you match each operatic character at left to his or her title?

1. Simon Boccanegra
2. Federica *Luisa Miller*
3. Don Julien *Don Rodrigo*
4. Hermann *Tannhäuser*
5. Rodrigo *Don Carlo*
6. Don Pedro *La Périchole*
7. Don Magnifico *La Cenerentola*
8. Lucrezia Borgia
9. Charles Blount *Gloriana*
10. Robert le Diable
11. Ishmael *Nabucco*
12. Paul *La Grande Duchesse de Gérolstein*
13. The Marschallin *Der Rosenkavalier*
14. Amfortas *Parsifal*
15. Dom Sebastian

a. Governor of Ceuta
b. Marquis of Posa
c. Duchess of Ferrara
d. Duchess of Ostheim
e. Duke of Normandy
f. Doge of Genoa
g. Prince of Stein-Stein-Steis-Laper-Bott-Moll-Schorstenburg
h. King of Portugal
i. Princess of Werdenberg
j. Governor of Lima
k. Lord Mountjoy
l. King of Monsalvat
m. Baron of Montefiascone
n. Landgrave of Thuringia
o. King of Jerusalem

Extra Credit:

A. What political apointment does Count Almaviva say he has received, in *Le Nozze di Figaro*?

B. Who are Linetta, Nicoletta, and Ninetta?

C. In *Mignon*, Philine is invited to a celebration in whose honor?

75. THE BAKER'S DOZEN

In what operas are the following "menus" featured?

1. Hens, marinades, buns, pastry, candy, vanilla, coffee
2. Eggs, ham, mustard, cress, strawberry jam, muffins, toast, Sally Lunn, a "rollicking" bun
3. A little venison, a superb pate, a succulent pudding
4. Turkey, ham, gravy, French-fried potatoes, plum pudding, cheese, pie, nuts
5. Six pullets, three turkeys, two pheasants, one anchovy
6. Hors d'oeuvres, spices, fish, chicken, crayfish, duck pate
7. Bacon, butter, flour, sausages, eggs, beans, onions, coffee
8. Chocolate layercake, marzipan, carob, rice pudding, cream, raisins, almonds, figs
9. Spring onions, leeks, watercress, cabbages, sage, fowl, a ham, sausages, salted meats
10. Oil, hazelnuts, walnut bread, flour, cheese, lentils, eggs, butter, currants
11. Roasted stag, a turkey, lobster
12. Jelly, pink blancmange, iced seedy cake, treacle tart, sausage rolls, trifle, chicken, ham, cheese straws, marzipan
13. Cakes, jellies, custard, chocolate dates, fruit salad, trifle, cream-filled pastries, almond favors

Extra Credit:

A. In what opera does a chorus feasting on turkey ask who wants to be served the "pope's nose"?

B. In what opera does a family rhapsodize over an omelette?

C. In what opera is there a character called Tapioca?

76. A MUSICAL GAZETEER

The places at left do not necessarily become the settings of, yet are mentioned in, the works at right. Match them up.

1. The Pindus Mountains
2. Knightsbridge
3. South Kensington Station
4. Mount Etna
5. Tremorden Castle
6. Poland
7. Castiglion Prison
8. The Peronnet Bridge
9. Guadalquivir
10. Milan
11. Armenia
12. Borgognone
13. The South Pacific
14. La Musée d'Artillerie
15. Montauban

a. *The Mikado*
b. *The Pirates of Penzance*
c. *La Rondine*
d. *Andrea Chénier*
e. *Les Contes d'Hoffmann*
f. *La Vie Parisienne*
g. *Lulu*
h. *Iolanthe*
i. *The Sorcerer*
j. *Mosé in Egitto*
k. *Manon*
l. *Rigoletto*
m. *Fedora*
n. *Don Quichotte*

Extra Credit:

A. Ping, Pang, and Pong own property—respectively, a house on a lake, a garden, and forests. Where are they located?

B. Act IV of an Italian opera is titled "The Orfano Canal." Name the opera.

C. What operatic heroine snarls, *"Al diavolo l'America!"* ("To hell with America!")?

77. GIFT HORSES

Gifts abound in opera. How generously can you answer the following questions?

1. What does Harry give Minnie in *La Fanciulla del West*?

2. Who once owned—or so he says—the jewels that Horace Tabor gives Baby Doe as a wedding gift.

3. How many louis does Violetta tell Annina to give to the poor?

4. What did Prince Obolowsky give Baba the Turk?

5. What was Don Basilio once given to wear, to teach him a lesson, as he relates in *Le Nozze di Figaro*?

6. What does Elisabeth of Valois give to a woman who has lost her two sons in battle?

7. What character in a crossover work reminisces about her old love affairs, one of which netted her a "tiny Titian"?

8. In *Simon Boccanegra*, what area has the King of Tartarca opened to Genoan fishing vessel as a gesture of peace?

9. Who promises Bergdorf Goodman clothes to a girl he'd like to seduce?

10. What gift does Golaud promise Yniold for spying on Pelléas and Mélisande?

11. What did Mandryka once do to please a lady-friend who had wanted to go sleigh-riding in July?

12. What is Andrew's anniversary gift to Abbie, in *Lizzie Borden*?

13. Who buys Lodoletta red wooden shoes as a birthday gift?

14. What is Nellie's Christmas gift to Alma in *Summer and Smoke*?

15. What is the Prince's gift to Philine in *Mignon*?

Extra Credit:

A. Arabella has three suitors: Count Elemer, Dominik, and Lamoral. Name the gift each man brings her.

B. Who is offered, among other treasures, chrysolites, beryls, rubies, and chalcedona to divert her attention from another attraction?

C. Albert Herring is given three prizes for being King of the May. What are they?

78. THE PITS

Conductors are, of course, indispensible to opera performances. How knowledgeable are you about recent leaders in the field?

1. Who is Maestro Carlos Kleiber's conductor-father?

2. What French conductor made his Met debut at the age of seventy-four, leading a performance of *Samson et Dalila*?

3. What conductor, associated with the Philadelphia Orchestra and Teatro alla Scala, will not work with singers who interpolate high notes?

4. What conductor discovered over one thousand missing pages of *Les Contes d'Hoffmann* and produced his restoration of this work in 1980 in Miami?

5. What conductor, who has led operas internationally, started out at the University of Tennessee as a premed student?

6. What Italian conductor holds an M.A. in psychiatry?

7. Which of the world's foremost conductors of Wagner did not make his Bayreuth conducting debut until the age of seventy?

8. What American maestra served as the Frankfurt Opera's principal conductor in addition to being the first woman to conduct opera at Teatro La Fenice in Venice?

9. What maestra never conducted the Minnesota Opera while she was their music director?

10. Zubin Mehta made his U.S. conducting debut at the podium of what opera production?

11. What conductor, making his New York City Opera debut that night, called for an unauthorized encore of one of the numbers in *La Rondine*?

12. What soprano walked out of the Met's *La Bohème* because she objected to the conducting of Eugene Kohn?

13. What conductor composed an opera entitled *Lou Salome*?

14. What American conductor became the Intendant of the Vienna Staatsoper in 1972?

15. Who was the music director of New York City Opera between Christopher Keene's employment in that position and Mr. Keene's ascent to general manager of the company?

Extra Credit:

A. What American conductor was invited in 1982 to lead the Central Opera Company of Peking's *La Traviata*—on its home ground?

B. What conductor took to Broadway in a production of *The Threepenny Opera* starring rock singer Sting?

C. How old was James Levine when he made his conducting debut at the Met?

79. A MUSICAL BOUQUET

If they're lucky, opera singers receive floral tributes from adoring fans. The characters they play are also not unacquainted with plants and blossoms.

1. In what kind of grove is the first scene of *Mireille* set?

2. What flower does Cio-Cio-San place in her hair as she awaits Pinkerton's return?

3. What tree does Walther sing about as he demonstrates his Prize Song to Hans Sachs at Hans's workshop?

4. During *Street Scene*, Sam and Rose sing a song set to a Walt Whitman poem about what kind of plant?

5. What centerpiece does Erika order for the dinner table, as *Vanessa* opens?

6. In what opera does adding an enameled rose to her clothing allow one woman to pass as another?

7. What flowers does Lulu wear in the bodice of her evening gown in Act II Scene 1 of *Lulu*?

8. What flowers does Mrs. Lovett decide she will place in Sweeney Todd's room to cheer it up?

9. What flowers adorn the costume of the Queen of the Fairies in Verdi's *Falstaff*?

10. What poisonous plant does Lakmé nibble on?

11. In *Le Jongleur de Notre-Dame*, Boniface sings about a simple plant that opened to form a cradle for the infant Jesus. What plant was this?

12. In what kind of tree does Mélisande's hair become entangled?

13. What herbal essence does Kundry use to heal Amfortas's wound?

14. What kind of flowers does Suzel bring her friend Fritz on his birthday?

15. What flower does Walter sing about, in *La Wally*?

Extra Credit:

A. What kind of wood was the magic flute carved from?

B. In *The Making of the Representative for Planet 8*, several characters journey to an icy region in search of what plant?

C. Why does Sophie sniff at the Silver Rose?

80. PERSONAL REFERENCES

The following people are spoken of, but do not appear, in their respective operas. Can you name these characters?

1. Albert Herring's aunt

2. The sage whose proverbs Suzuki quotes to Pinkerton

3. William Jennings Bryan's political opponent in *The Ballad of Baby Doe*

4. The adventuress who betrayed Ramerrez in *La Fanciulla del West*

5. The first apprentice to die while in Peter Grimes's service

6. The Biblical figure to whom Eva compares Walther when she sees him in church

7. Cassio's girlfriend, in Verdi's *Otello*

8. Ortrud's father

9. Suor Angelica's younger sister

10. The Irish rebel Elizabeth I hopes to overthrow, in *Gloriana*

11. The religious figure to whom le Comte des Grieux sarcastically compares his son

12. The name under which Madeleine de Coigny will die in *Andrea Chénier*

13. The man for whom *Capriccio*'s ballet dancer will perform the next day

14. The woman Robert Storch is falsely accused of having an affair with, in *Intermezzo*

15. The woman to whom Dr. Schön is engaged in *Lulu*

Extra Credit:

A. With whom are Wilhelm, Hermann, and Nathanael in love, in *Les Contes d'Hoffmann*?

B. Who were Pagliaccio, Mezzetino, Cavicchino, Burattin, and Pasquariello?

C. In what operetta are the names of Lord Nelson, Fielding, Queen Anne, Mr. Micawber, and Madame Tussaud—among others—linked in a song?

81. ACTION!

No matter how old an opera is, a director will always find something new to do with it, as the following have illustrated:

1. The Met is the second company for whom Franco Zeffirelli has staged *La Bohème*. Name the first.

2. With what opera company did Renata Scotto make her directorial debut in 1987?

3. What director has earned the nickname "the bad boy of opera," for his updated stagings that have included *Le Nozze di Figaro* set in Trump Tower and *Tannhäuser* drawing televangelistic parallels?

4. What production marked Luciano Pavarotti's directorial debut?

5. With what opera company did Jonathan Miller make his U.S. directorial debut?

6. Who staged Bayreuth's 1983 *Ring* cycle?

7. Who both conducted and directed New York City Opera's 1976 televised *Il Barbiere di Siviglia*?

8. What was filmmaker Lina Wertmuller's first attempt at staging live opera?

9. What was Harold Prince's first Met production?

10. What soprano, called the "Callas of Soubrettes," turned to directing in the 1980s, for such companies as the San Francisco Opera and the Met?

11. What director's trademark was a palette of neutral colors (though his *Manon* dressed its heroine in fiery red)?

12. What opera did mezzo-soprano Regina Resnik stage in her directorial debut in 1971?

13. What Swedish director made his Met debut staging a double bill of *Duke Bluebeard's Castle* and *Erwartung*?

14. Who created a ninety-minute version of Bizet's opera, called *La Tragédie de Carmen*?

15. What Argentinian director became the general manager of the Pittsburgh Opera in the early 1960s?

Extra Credit:

A. What opera director was host of a TV science series called "The Body in Question"?

B. What Iranian staging and opera company director was delivered stillborn but then revived, resulting in his being named "Kindness of God" in his native tongue?

C. Whose 1988 New York City Opera staging of *Rasputin* included nude male and female actors portraying the monk's followers?

82. SONDHEIM

In the world of musical theater, there are "Sondheimites" and "Weberites." Though the latter's *Phantom of the Opera* is a big hit, it is the former's works that are making their way into opera houses, in a crossover move unusual for occurring during the composer/lyricist's own lifetime.

1. What was the first opera company to stage *Sweeney Todd* in 1984?

2. What singer—who appeared in the original Broadway cast, though not initially in this role—sang the part of Anthony Hope in the above staging?

3. What operatic baritone played *Sweeney Todd* in the work's debut on the opera stage?

4. In *Sweeney Todd*, there is a joke about the difference between Italianate and Irish tenors. What operatic tenor created the role of Pirelli on Broadway?

5. What film of a Sondheim work—released in 1978 and poorly reviewed—won an Academy Award for its Adaptation Score?

6. Who wrote the above adaptation, and is closely associated with Stephen Sondheim as orchestrator of many of his shows?

7. What conductor has led the majority of Stephen Sondheim's shows on Broadway, as well as New York City Opera performances of *Sweeney Todd* and *A Little Night Music*?

8. What is unusual about the score of *A Little Night Music*, as compared to other musical theater works of its era?

9. What composer/conductor is name-dropped in "The Ladies Who Lunch" in *Company*?

10. In "Remember?" from *A Little Night Music*, an opera is named as having been "belched" by a boatman during a romantic rendezvous. Name the opera.

11. What coloratura soprano sang the role of "Young Heidi" in the New York Philharmonic concert performance of *Follies* recorded in 1985?

12. Who sang the part of the mature Heidi at that same performance?

13. What British opera company produced and recorded *Pacific Overtures* in 1987?

14. On what recording can Stephen Sondheim be heard accompanying a singer's rendition of "Send in the Clowns"?

15. On what recording can one hear the composer himself singing one of his own compositions?

Extra Credit:

A. Name the five "Liebeslieder" characters in *A Little Night Music.*

B. What university faculty did Stephen Sondheim join in 1990, as its first Cameron Mackintosh Professor of Contemporary Theatre?

C. What is Adolfo Pirelli's real name?

83. NO PLACE LIKE HOME

Match the household objects at left to the opera in which they are named.

1. Wicker chair	a. *H.M.S. Pinafore*
2. Dustbin	b. *La Rondine*
3. [Laundry] basket	c. *La Bohème*
4. Band-Aids	d. *Albert Herring*
5. A nail	e. *La Gazza Ladra*
6. Ladder	f. *The Last Savage*
7. Screen	g. *Falstaff*
8. Gridiron	h. *Sweeney Todd*
9. Kitchen faucet	i. *L'Enfant et les Sortilèges*
10. Oriental rugs	j. *Vanessa*
11. Stair-railing	k. *Werther*
12. Wallpaper	l. *Der Freischütz*
13. Silver spoon	m. *Rigoletto*
14. Mirrors	n. *Street Scene*
15. Harpsichord	o. *La Pomme d'Api*

Extra Credit:

A. What operatic family gets dispossessed during *Street Scene*?

B. What operatic character says that she hasn't sat down in a room with curtains, a sofa, and pictures for two years?

C. Which opera opens with a command concerning the placement of a blue sofa?

84. MICRO AND MACRO

Science, from the splitting of the atom to the wonders of the universe, plays a part in a number of operas.

1. In what Haydn opera is a man, transported merely to another's garden, duped into thinking he has gone to the moon?

2. In whose opera is the moon stolen from the sky?

3. Who puts it back?

4. Upon whose novel of the same title is *The Making of the Representative for Planet 8* based?

5. Who composed it?

6. In whose Spoleto Festival USA staging of *Madama Butterfly*—set in World War II Nagasaki—did a simulated atom bomb explosion conclude the opera?

7. Robert Ward composed an opera about the responsibilities of a nuclear physicist. Name the opera.

8. Who wrote its libretto?

9. What is the name of a Janáček opera in which a burgher, in a drunken stupor, travels back in time to the 1400s and also visits the moon?

10. For his seventieth birthday, what space-age opera did Gian Carlo Menotti compose?

11. What Offenbach operetta is based upon a Jules Verne story?

12. What Menotti opera concerns a schoolbus attacked by aliens?

13. What frightens the creatures away?

14. Who composed an operetta entitled *Frau Luna*?

15. In that work, how do the characters ascend to the moon?

Extra Credit:

A. What Gilbert and Sullivan character claims that he can trace his family back to "a protoplasmal primordial atomic globule"?

B. In *Street Scene*, what is described as being three parts high octane and one part atom bomb?

C. What is considered the world's first opera inspired by the modern space age?

85. CONSECRATED PLACES

Can you match these religious structures to the operas they relate to?

1. The monastery of St. Just	a. *Lizzie Borden*
	b. *La Forza del Destino*
2. St. Sulpice	c. *La Gioconda*
3. The convent of the Madonna degli Angeli	d. *Manon*
	e. *Tosca*
4. The Cathedral of Toledo	f. *Lodoletta*
	g. *Don Carlo*
5. Old Harbor Church	h. *Don Rodrigo*
6. San Marco Church	i. *La Battaglia di Legnano*
7. Nostra Donna d'Atocha	j. *I Lombardi*
8. Church of Sain' Angelo della Valle	
9. Saint Ambrogio Church	
10. Saint Guido's	

Extra Credit:

A. What does the title character in *The Saint of Bleecker Street* take as her name when she becomes a nun?

B. How many angels do Hansel and Gretel believe watch over them?

C. What is the name of the congregation sponsoring the picnic in *Porgy and Bess*?

86. BREAK A LEG

Part of the excitement of attending live opera is being on the scene when the unexpected happens. Were you there for these performer mishaps, cancellations, and substitutions?

1. When *Semiramide* was performed as part of Carnegie Hall's Gala Rossini Opera Festival on 1/10/83, who replaced the indisposed Monserrat Caballé in the title role?

2. What Irish mezzo made her Met debut on 10/18/84 in *La Clemenza di Tito*—not as the scheduled Annio, but substituting for Tatiana Troyanos in the role of Sesto?

3. By the time that the English National Opera had reached the last day of its 1984 U.S. tour, illness and fatigue had felled some of its performers. On this final day, 6/30/84, who sang Robert Deveraux in the matinee performance of *Gloriana* and also performed the Duke of Mantua that evening?

4. On 1/7/69, the show at the Houston Grand Opera—a *Barbiere*—nearly didn't go on when its Bartolo, Andrew Foldi, succumbed to the flu and no cover was in the house. What bass volunteered to go on, and performed the role with score in hand?

5. What Wagnerian soprano was sent off to the hospital by a falling (luckily, lightweight foam) beam during the 4/28/90 Met performance of *Götterdämmerung*?

6. What soprano—hired only as a cover for the season—made headlines for substituting for Anna Somowa-Sintow in *Simon Boccanegra* and for Monserrat Caballe in *Ernani* during her first Met season?

7. On 11/29/85, in a Connecticut State Opera performance of *The Consul*, what mezzo was pressed into singing both The Mother and The Secretary?

8. On 10/20/86, what Met Tosca suffered a jaw injury when her scarpia, Juan Pons, became a little too energetic during Act II?

9. What soprano, attending the show merely as part of the audience, wound up singing Act II through the finale of *La Traviata* after Carol Vaness, in her debut in that role with the company, became too ill to finish singing Act I?

10. What soprano took over from the same place in 1987 after Gianna Rolandi, coincidentally also making her debut in that role with the company, sang only to the end of Act I?

11. Who rescued the San Francisco Opera's opening night *Otello* on 12/10/83—three and one-half hours after the curtain had been scheduled to go up—by flying in to replace the indisposed Carlo Cossutta?

12. What bass made his unscheduled New York City Opera debut as Giorgio Walton in 1981, because Justino Diaz, the second-cast artist who would otherwise be covering that role, needed to save his voice for *Nabucco*, also being performed by the company during that period?

13. On 10/20/85, Mirella Freni and Plácido Domingo both pulled out of the opening night production at the Houston Grand Opera, and were replaced by Fiamma Izzo d'Amico and Giacomo Aragall. What was the opera?

14. What heldentenor cancelled his 1983 San Diego Opera *Lohengrin* engagement because he needed to have his tonsils removed?

15. Rockwell Blake sang only Act I of the 12/16/86 performance of the Met's *I Puritani*, then withdrew due to illness. Who took over the role of Arturo in Act III, in his company debut?

Extra Credit:

A. On 10/13/82, tenor Carlo Bini set off boos when he replaced Plácido Domingo in a Met *La Gioconda*. Though Bini braved out the evening, his conductor did not. Who conducted Acts I through III, and who then took over at the podium to finish the opera?

B. Which two tenors named Neil both called in sick for the 3/18/89 Met radio broadcast of *Werther*—and which *third* Neil went on in the title role?

C. The Met's 9/25/84 *Les Contes d'Hoffmann* had a unique turnaround: instead of starring one leading tenor and three leading ladies, it had one soprano as Hoffmann's loves—and three tenors as Hoffmann. Name the three "poets" who held the evening together.

87. IT'S GREEK TO ME

The lines at left occur in works that are otherwise primarily sung in another language. These extracts range from French and Latin to Japanese and even Greek! Can you match them to their operas?

1. *"Misera me"*
2. *"Quod erat demonstratum"*
3. *"Addio, mia vita, addio"*
4. *"De profundis . . ."*
5. *"Le chapeau Pamela"*
6. *"Tales Patris, talem Filias"*
7. *"Largo, largo! Pizzicato, pizzicato!"*
8. *"Sic itur ad astra"*
9. *"Wir wollen essen!"*
10. *"Ploremus"*
11. *"O ni! bikkuri shakkuri to!"*
12. *"Buon' giorno, signorine!"*
13. *"O Kami! O Kami!"*
14. *"Evoe"*
15. *"La Gloire c'est tout"*

a. *Capriccio*
b. *I Vespri Siciliani*
c. *La Forza del Destino*
d. *Sapho*
e. *Owen Wingrave*
f. *Madama Butterfly*
g. *Candide*
h. *The Mikado*
i. *Der Rosenkavalier*
j. *Casanova*
k. *La Vie Parisienne*
l. *La Cenerentola*
m. *The Gondoliers*
n. *Orphée aux Enfers*

Extra Credit:

A. In what Massenet opera is a song performed in Provencal dialect?

B. In *Der Rosenkavalier*, which character speaks with Baron Ochs in a mixture of German and Italian?

C. In what French opera does a string of Oriental nonsense phrases include the name "Sessue Hayakawa"?

88. BARGAIN BASEMENT

Opera plots sometimes include scenes with street vendors, or other instances of items being bought or sold.

1. In what opera are cakes, handkerchiefs, bananas, betel leaves, mats, honeycombs, and slippers sold at a marketplace?

2. In what opera are leeks, turnips, prunes, strawberries, cream cheese, cabbage, and green sauce hawked by vendors?

3. In what opera do open-air salespeople offer slippers, rouge, beauty spots, ruffles, kerchiefs, hoods, songs, lottery tickets, powder, tobacco graters, ribbons, cane, and hats?

4. In what opera do early-morning greengrocers sell carrots, watercress, peas, birdseed, and artichokes?

5. Who offers for sale barometers, hygrometers, thermometers . . . and eyes?

6. In what work do vendors' wares include waffles, oysters, peas, asparagus, and potatoes?

7. It's Christmas eve, but in what opera are the following still on sale for people who need to complete their holiday shopping: orange trees, dates, hot chestnuts, trinkets, caramels, coconut milk, and sparrows?

8. In what opera does a woman buy devil-crabs from a vendor, and other people announce their merchandise as being honey and strawberries?

9. In what Weill work is a drugstore lauded for its selection of hot and cold food, including chicken hash, chop suey, and banana splits?

10. In what Sondheim work are a patent elixir and meat pies sold to the same melody?

Extra Credit:

A. In what opera are the contents of a house put up for auction and, accidentally, the lady of the house as well?

B. In what Verdi opera do characters sell their jewelry *to* a peddler?

C. What twentieth century one-act French opera concerns a man who tries to sell his wife, but even the devil sends her back as a bad bargain?

89. THE PEANUT GALLERY, PART I

"There is more of a Sublime in the snare-drum part of *La Gazza Ladra* than in the whole of the *Ninth Symphony*."
—Thomas Pynchon, *Gravity's Rainbow*

Below, comments that famous composers have made about others who have written operas. Can you identify the subject? For extra credit, give the originator of the remarks.

1. "_____ is France's greatest composer, alas. A musician of great genius, a little talent."

2. You were the beginnings of my life as an artist. I sprang from you. You are the cause and I am the consequence."

3. "_____ is sunshine."

4. "_____ has a sense of timing and punctuation which I have never been able to find a Richard Strauss."

5. "Something like a court composer to Kaiser Wilhelm II."

6. "_____'s music reminds me of a blissful, eternally youthful life before the Fall."

7. "He would do better to shovel snow instead of scribbling on music paper."

8. "_____ is obviously mad."

9. "He wrote marvelous operas, but dreadful music."

10. "Such an outstanding lack of talent was never before united to such pretentiousness."

11. "My cook understands more about counterpoint than he does."

12. "The Mozart of the Champs-Élysées."

13. "His music exasperates sometimes, but it never bores."

14. "Amazingly modern and, if one can say such a thing, near to me in spirit."

15. "He was the greatest composer that ever lived."

90. THE PEANUT GALLERY, PART II

"Direct *Salome* and *Elektra* as if they had been written by Mendelssohn. Elfin music."

—Richard Strauss

Which operas are discussed in the following quotes? For extra credit, identify the composers whose opinions are being expressed.

1. "I liked the opera very much. Everything but the music."

2. "It was painful from start to finish."

3. "A libretto that should never have been accepted on a subject that never should have been chosen [by] a man who should never have attempted it."

4. "The only perfect English opera ever written."

5. "Very commonplace, vulgar, and uninteresting."

6. "Truly, let us thank heaven that nothing worse can come after this."

7. "While listening to it all I thought of those lovely princesses in Sacher Masoch who lavished upon their young men the most voluptuous kisses while drawing red-hot irons over their lovers' ribs."

8. "Marionette stage-music!"

9. "[Its composer] wrote the first and last acts of _____. God wrote the second."

10. "I heard _____ for the first time after the war and I confess I prefer Gilbert and Sullivan."

11. "How sublimely classical."

12. "It's organ grinder's stuff."

13. "I could not compose operas like _____ and _____. I hold them both in aversion."

14. "If that was music, I have never understood what music was."

15. "A sort of chromatic moan."

91. NOT NECESSARILY FOR YOUNG EARS

The operas at left are each based upon a children's story or fairy tale. Can you match each work to its composer at right?

1. *Higglety Pigglety Pop!*   a. Barab
2. *Little Red Riding Hood*   b. Glass
3. *Babar the Elephant*   c. Rossini
4. *The Emperor's New*   d. Knussen
   Clothes   e. Stravinsky
5. *Cardillac*   f. Goldmark
6. *The Juniper Tree*   g. Bereznowsky
7. *Where the Wild Things*   h. Moore
   Are   i. Hindemith
8. *The Cricket on the*
   Hearth
9. *La Cenerentola*
10. *Le Rossignol*

Extra Credit:

A. What internationally-famous diva starred in a TV series called "Who's Afraid of Opera"?

B. What were the names of her three puppet costars?

C. What children's book illustrator has designed productions of such operas as *The Love for Three Oranges* and *The Cunning Little Vixen*?

92. MET TRIVIA, PART I

How "up" are you on Met lore?

1. What was the first native-born American to perform a principal role at the Met?

2. Who was the founder of the Metropolitan Opera Guild?

3. What millionaire Met box-holder, after the work's U.S. premiere, demanded that *Salome* be destroyed because of its profanity?

4. What was the Met's first radio broadcast to feature Milton Cross?

5. What opera did New York's 11/9/65 blackout switch off from taking place?

6. With what production did Alfred Lunt make his Met debut as staging director, in 1951?

7. What J.C. Bach cantata, sometimes performed as an opera, was first performed at the Met in 1942?

8. What was the last season that the Met cancelled in its entirety?

9. Opening night at the Met's 1918–1919 season also marked the end of World War I: 11/11/18. What was the opera that night?

10. When was the first live radio broadcast from the Met?

11. In 1933, whose twenty-fifth year of association with the Met was celebrated with a gala performance in which every artist on the company roster appeared onstage?

12. What baritone, who joined the Met in 1926, delayed his retirement from singing in order to be able to perform during the final season at the old house—at the age of seventy-three?

13. During the early 1930s, the Met season was not complete without a special performance in each season featuring company stars doing both serious numbers and specially-written comic skits. In 1935, one piece of the program was called "Nibelungen Ringling Brothers-Barnum Bailey & *Götterdämmerung*." What was the name of this kind of Met event?

14. The Met has not been without nepotism. During one season, who silently portrayed the Queen of Shemakh onstage as coloratura soprano Maria Barrientos sang the role from the pit?

15. On what date was the Met Centennial Gala?

Extra Credit:

A. What three Met productions were staged by George Ballanchine?

B. What was the first opera by a U.S.-born composer to be performed on opening night of the Met's New York season, in 1933—and what other opera had already been performed at that afternoon's matinee?

C. The Met's first season consisted of operas sung exclusively in one language, and its second season of operas sung only in another (in both cases, these included works performed in translation). Name the two languages.

93. MET TRIVIA, PART II

1. What was the first Handel opera to be performed by the Met, on 1/19/84?

2. What acrobatic troupe was engaged to perform its battle scene?

3. What scheduled opera was cancelled in order to produce the Texaco 50th Anniversary Concert on 3/10/90?

4. Who is the first performer to be made a managing director of the Met?

5. On 12/11/52, what Met performance was broadcast live to movie theaters across the country?

6. What opera was dropped during the Met's 1941–1942 season, not to reappear until 1946, because of American sentiment regarding an event of World War II?

7. Frederica von Stade and Nicolai Gedda sang the Met's first recital-style concert under the company's music directorship of James Levine. Who accompanied them at the piano?

8. Whose idea was the Mini-Met, the one-season program for developing artists?

9. What was the first opera to be televised live from the Met?

10. In what theater did the Met's first performance at Lincoln Center take place?

11. What singer made his U.S. recital debut on the Met stage in 1989?

12. During the 1952–1953 season, what opera was given at the Met in two versions, Italian and English?

13. What was the first opera performed in the Metropolitan Opera House at Lincoln Center?

14. What baritone made his Met debut during the 1985–1986 season as Falstaff, at the age of sixty-nine?

15. What Met-sponsored project, which lasted only two years, included an evening of modern pieces sung by Ella Fitzgerald, another night devoted to Latin American music, and another consisting of British works, among other programs?

Extra Credit:

A. Name the eight operas that the Met performed in May 1939 as their contribution to New York events relating to the World's Fair.

B. Name the "troika" of directors—and their titles—chosen to manage the Met's 1975–1976 season.

C. In 1954, the Met's opening night consisted of scenes from four Italian operas rather than of one complete, long work. Name the operatic selections.

94. ACROSS THE PLAZA

In New York operatic jargon, when one has just been speaking of the Met, "across the plaza" means New York City Opera (and vice versa)—a mock-genteel way of referring to these rivaling companies based at the same arts complex, Lincoln Center.

1. What was the first production of New York City Opera's national company (its touring division)?

2. During the fall 1952 and fall 1953 seasons, New York City Opera collaborated with what foreign company to produce a bilingual *Madama Butterfly*?

3. What New York City Opera "Summer Festival" never took place because its orchestra went on strike to protest having a summer season?

4. The daughter of a famous New York City Opera portrayor of demons made her company debut as, appropriately, the wraithlike Miss Jessel in the ghost-story opera *The Turn of the Screw*. Name her.

5. During New York City Opera's 1976 "Operathon" radio broadcast, the company performed excerpts from a bel canto work that has never otherwise been part of their repertory. Name it.

6. Who conducted the American premiere of *The Voice of Ariadne* at New York City Opera in 1977?

7. What opera was presented by the company in both English and Italian versions during its fall 1972 season?

8. What is the only New York City Opera production to date staged by Jerome Robbins?

9. What soprano made her company debut as Violetta in a performance that has been dubbed by opera fanatics as "the scream *Traviata*"—not because of the sounds coming from the stage, but as a result of the unexpected, bloodcurdling shriek let loose by a member of the audience at the beginning of Act II?

10. In what New York City Opera performance did Victoria de los Angeles make her only company appearance?

11. When did New York City Opera's warehouse fire, in which costumes for seventy-four productions were destroyed, take place?

12. What New York City Opera production featured Joel Grey in a leading role?

13. Arleen Augér's only appearances with the company were in 1969. What was her debut role with the troupe?

14. What West Coast opera company had a fifteen-year association with New York City Opera during Beverly Sill's performing years?

15. On 11/7/81, an elderly attendee of a New York City Opera matinee fell to her death from the topmost tier of the theater. What opera had ended only moments before?

Extra Credit:

A. Name the six New York City Opera general directors since the company's creation.

B. Name the three works and composers that comprised the company's 10/9/80 world premiere of "An American Trilogy."

C. Name the five shows presented in the company's 1986 through 1990 spring musical comedy season.

95. THE PRINTED PAGE

While newspapers and magazines are most commonly associated with opera with regard to reviews, there are also other connections between publications and the stage.

1. What operatic charcter is ordered by her father to read the newspaper aloud to him?

2. Who reads to the Marschallin from a scandal sheet?

3. In *Street Scene*, which character rails against the "capitalist press"?

4. In that same work, who sings a lullaby interspersed with a discussion of a tabloid article on the double murder that occurs during the opera?

5. What newspaper does Aschenbach buy, in *Death in Venice*?

6. When the Painter in *Lulu* commits suicide, Lulu tells Dr. Schön that the news is worthy of putting out an extra edition of his paper. What headline does Dr. Schön propose?

7. In what opera is a newspaper ad for a farmhand read aloud?

8. What is the name of the newspaper vendor in *The Saint of Bleecker Street*?

9. What is the only way she expects to ever see her own picture in a paper?

10. In *La Grande Duchesse de Gérolstein*, a gazette of what nationality is quoted from by Prince Paul?

11. What newspaper does Rodolfo lay as a tablecloth in *La Bohème*?

12. For what publication does he need to complete an article?

13. One of Rossini's rare failures concerns a Neapolitan man who places an ad in a Parisian newspaper in hopes of finding a husband for his daughter. Name the opera.

14. What New York opera critic sang minor tenor roles with New York City Opera from 1958 through 1960?

15. What composer, winner of a Grand Prix de Rome, wrote music criticism for the *Journal des Débats* and the *Gazette Musicale* in order to make ends meet?

Extra Credit:

Name all five newspapers represented by reporters in *Captain Jinks of the Horse Marines*.

96. AGE DISCRIMINATION

In opera, characters' ages are rarely crucial to the plot and yet, when supplied, they help fill out characters' personalities considerably.

1. In *Chérubin*, how old is the title character?

2. How old is Wowkle's baby?

3. In Massenet's *Manon*, how old is the title character in Act II?

4. In Puccini's *Manon Lescaut*, how old is the character said to be during Act II?

5. How old was Lulu when Dr. Schön met her?

6. What birthday does Frederic celebrate at the start of *The Pirates of Penzance*?

7. How old is Pirate Ruth?

8. How old is Antonia in *Les Contes d'Hoffmann*?

9. How old is Cio-Cio-San at the time of her marriage?

10. How old is Gianni Schicchi?

11. How old is Red Whiskers, in *Billy Budd*?

12. How old is Magda Sorel, in *The Consul*?

13. What age does the disguised Papagena tell Papageno that she is?

14. How old is the Grand Inquisitor, in *Don Carlo*?

15. At what age does Iolanthe appear to have given birth to Strephon, by human calculation?

Extra Credit:

Match these characters to their ages:

A. Zita in *Gianni Schicchi*	a. 25
B. Simone in *Gianni Schicchi*	b. 22
	c. 60
C. Nella in *Gianni Schicchi*	d. 70
D. Miss Wordsworth in *Albert Herring*	e. 38
	f. 26
E. Albert in *Albert Herring*	g. 49
F. Nancy in *Albert Herring*	h. 45
G. Casanova in *Casanova*	
H. Lorenzo in *Casanova*	

97. FUN AND GAMES

Operatic characters have their hobbies too.

1. What sport does Sam play in the gym, in *Trouble in Tahiti*?

2. In Act I of *Albert Herring*, why do the three children enter the greengrocer's?

3. At Flora's party in *La Traviata*, a song is sung about a toreador. How many bulls must he kill in one day in order for his sweetheart to accept his proposal?

4. In *Antony and Cleopatra*, who calls for a game of billiards?

5. What Berlioz opera contains a pantomimed hunting scene set in an African forest?

6. What verismo opera contains a song called the "Bicycle Aria"?

7. What opera ends with a choral salute to Olympic athletes?

8. At the start of Act II of *Le Roi de Lahore*, what game are the guards engaged in?

9. In what opera is there javelin and discus throwing?

10. What Offenbach work contains a word game that ultimately spells out "locomotive"?

Extra Credit:

A. What are the names of the child soloists who imitate Park Avenue types during *Street Scene*'s "Street Games" ensemble?

B. In Leoncavallo's *La Bohème*, who deliberately loses at pool so that the money he pays up will cover the bohemians' dinner bill?

C. What American composer, generally only listed as having written two operas, also composed a chamber opera entitled *A Hand of Bridge*?

98. MAGIC WORDS

One often speaks of the magic of opera—here are some examples of magic *in* opera.

1. In what nineteenth century American opera is one aria totally comprised of a list of folk superstitions?

2. What operatic character kisses a rabbit's foot to have luck while gambling?

3. What sacred plant does Norma use in her ceremonies?

4. In what Handel opera does a character, based on the historical figure Godfrey of Bouillon, use a magic wand to turn an enchanted garden into a desert?

5. What is the name of the magician in *The Consul*?

6. In *Cendrillon*, where does the Fairy Queen live?

7. How is Faust able to fly, in *Mefistofele*?

8. In Gilbert and Sullivan's *The Sorcerer*, how is the love philtre administered?

9. What is John Wellington Wells's address?

10. What is the name of the witch in *Mireille*?

11. Who turned Godfrey of Brabant into a swan?

12. In *Das Rheingold*, what is the first creature that Alberich transforms himself into, at Loge's request?

13. In *Le Postillon de Longjumeau*, who read Chapelou's palm before he was married?

14. Who accidentally evokes the devil in *Grisélidis*?

15. When Sullivan refused to collaborate with Gilbert on an operetta about a magic lozenge, what composer did the librettist team up with in order to produce *The Mountebanks*?

Extra Credit:

A. In *The Rake's Progress*, Tom must name three cards drawn by Nick in order to break Nick's spell over him. What are his three correct answers?

B. In *The Sorcerer*, what does John Wellington Wells charge for casting a horoscope?

C. In that same work, what article of merchandise has he sold only one of recently, only to have it returned?

99. DOUBLE-BILLS, PART I

Earn double points on these last two quizzes of miscellaneous opera facts. Part I concerns music, lyrics, and singing.

1. In what language was *Lohengrin* first performed in New York?

2. For whom did Massenet rewrite the tenor line of *Werther* for baritone voice?

3. Who was the first North American to sing Boris Godunov in Moscow?

4. What is Zerbinetta's highest note in R. Strauss's original version of *Ariadne auf Naxos*?

5. In what Prokofiev opera is Faust a bass and Mephisto a tenor?

6. Who wrote the libretto for an ultimately uncomposed opera called *Doctor Faustus Lights the Lights*?

7. What opera, composed by Kittl, has a text by Richard Wagner?

8. *Il Trovatore* is notorious for having one of the most confusing plots in all of opera. Possibly part of its problem may stem from its librettist, Salvatore Cammarano, having died before completing his revisions. Who finished the job for him?

9. Who invented the glass harmonica, used to chilling effect in *Lucia di Lammermoor*?

10. What composer played Papageno in the first *Die Zauberflöte* to be performed in English in Great Britain?

11. What Victor Herbert opera contains music based upon Native America motifs?

12. What troupe commissioned it?

13. What Viennese Wagnerian mezzo started out an Italian-repertoire lyric soprano?

14. In 1982, Gian Carlo Menotti received Italy's highest artistic honor. What was it?

15. What Offenbach operetta is partially sung in fake Chinese?

Extra Credit:

A. In *Le Postillon de Longjumeau*, what high note of the title character does the Marquis de Corcy specifically compliment?

B. In Act II of *La Bohème*, Schaunard tries out a horn and tells its vendor that a particular note is off. Which note?

C. In *Il Viaggio a Reims*, in what key does the Baron Trombonok ask that the French anthem be sung?

100. DOUBLE-BILLS, PART II

Again, double points for these questions, this time concerning opera plots.

1. What opera opens with a description, complete with maps, of one of Napoleon's battles?

2. What brand of matches does Albert Herring seek when he comes home to a dark house?

3. In *L'Etoile du Nord*, Peter the Great—disguised as a humble carpenter—is asked his father's profession. What is his honest reply?

4. To what regiment does Marie belong?

5. What is Musetta's nickname for Alcindoro?

6. What phrase does Fiordiligi claim is symbolized by letters she sees in Dorabella's palm?

7. How is Figaro physically identified as the son of Dr. Bartolo and Marcellina?

8. What sex is Mélisande's child?

9. In what Rossini opera does an aria list such motley items as pearls, trombones, opium, and sables?

10. What college did Kitty, of *The Last Savage*, attend?

11. What is the name of the eunuch in *Antony and Cleopatra*?

12. In what Saint-Saëns opera does a man fall in love with a woman depicted on a Japanese scroll painting?

13. What Sullivan work contains a lullaby about bacon?

14. What opera, which premiered on NBC-TV in 1961, is about Mormon leader Brigham Young?

15. What is Don Geronio's horoscope sign?

Extra Credit:

A. What three types of cigars does Minnie offer the men in *La Fanciulla del West*?

B. Mascagni and Erlanger both wrote operatic works based upon the writing of author team Erckmann-Chatrian, and each on Jewish subjects. Name the operas.

C. What are the names of The Defendant and The Plaintiff in *Trial by Jury*?

Answers

Unless otherwise noted, score one point per answer in the main section of each quiz, and two points per answer in the extra credit section.

1650 to 2200 points: STANDING ROOM ONLY
You know more about opera than many music professionals! You not only deserve a torn-program confetti salute, but you know what it is!

1100 to 1650 points: BOX HOLDER
While you are clearly a devoted opera attendee or home listener, you still need to get over a few prejudices (hate new music? only consider international-level stars "real" singers?). To be truly rounded, take another look and listen to areas you are deliberately avoiding in the opera world.

550 to 1100 points: SUBSCRIBER
A good try! You love opera but now need to expand your horizons beyond tried and true works and artists. The first step: explore other operas by composers you enjoy and works written by their contemporaries, open your ears to other singers' interpretations of familiar pieces, and try a "wild card" now and then.

0 to 550 points: MATINEE MAVEN
You enjoy opera as an entertainment, but have just realized how vast and complex the subject is. Take heart! Everyone who scores higher began at your level. How to improve your score: increase your reading and listening in areas that, in these quizzes, have caught your interest. You'll be a buff in no time!

1. ANSWERS

1. Lalo.	9. Delibes.
2. Montemezzi.	10. Bizet.
3. Paulus.	11. Rimsky-Korsakov.
4. Donizetti.	12. Humperdinck.
5. Chabrier.	13. Massenet.
6. Rossini.	14. Saint-Saëns.
7. Glinka.	15. Gounod.
8. Musgrave.	

Extra Credit:

A. Boetia.
B. Anne Boleyn *Anna Bolena*, Mary Stuart *Maria Stuarda*, Elizabeth I *Roberto Deveraux*, the Queen of Shemakha *Le Coq d'Or*, the Queen of the Night *Die Zauberflöte*, and Juana *La Loca*.
C. *Un Giorno di Regno*.

*One point for each character name in B, two points each for A and C.

2. ANSWERS*

1. a, k	9. u, m
2. f, u	10. j, n
3. c, k	11. j, p
4. e, g	12. d, r
5. n, o	13. b, f
6. l, s	14. v, l
7. q, s	15. a, c
8. i, o	

Extra Credit:

A. iv
B. vi
C. i
D. v
E. ii
F. iii

*One point each for each letter answer to questions 1-15.

3. ANSWERS

1. e	9. m
2. d	10. h
3. l	11. e
4. j	12. i
5. i	13. k
6. a	14. f
7. b	15. g
8. c	

Extra Credit:

A. iii
B. i
C. v
D. ii
E. iv

4. ANSWERS*

All were considered failures at their premiers.

Extra Credit:

Menotti's *The Island God* was such a disaster that the composer quickly withdrew and destroyed most of its score. Only several orchestral passages and songs escaped obliteration.

*Ten points for the answer to the main body of the quiz; five points each for naming the extra credit opera and providing its reason.

5. ANSWERS

1. g	9. d
2. i	10. b
3. h	11. f
4. n	12. c
5. o	13. k
6. m	14. e
7. j	15. l
8. a	

Extra Credit:

A. They are half-brothers.
B. She is his foster sister.
C. It was composed by the brothers Luigi and Federico Ricci.

6. ANSWERS

1. k	9. n
2. e	10. i
3. h	11. d
4. a	12. j
5. o	13. m
6. f*	14. g
7. b	15. c
8. l	

Extra Credit:**

1. Elvira is heard singing a brief fragment of a love song that Arturo subsequently sings back to her in full.
2. Rodolfo's friends, calling to him from the street, retreat respectfully to the Café Momus when they learn that he has a lady visitor upstairs.
3. Manon hears the service at St. Sulpice and, inspired by the sound, soon sings her own fervent if somewhat selfish prayer.
4. Mario, undergoing torture in the next room, calls out his defiance to Scarpia.
5. As Tamino tries to enter the Masonic temple, voices tell him to turn back.
6. Known as the "Siciliana," this is Turiddu's clandestine serenade to Lola.
7. Violetta hears the revelers celebrating the Mardi Gras outside her window as she lies dying.
8. The townpeople gather to help the crew off Otello's ship.
9. Before the title character makes his appearance, an offstage chorus praises the angels.
10. Marguerite's rejection of Faust in her final moments grants her salvation, in the form of a heavenly pronouncement.
11. As Werther dies in Charlotte's arms, her young siblings sing a happy Christmas carol outside.

12. Nadir sings to Leila even as she prepares to spend the night alone in chaste and pious retreat.

13. We have our first taste of Lakmé's high soprano when she begins a prayer from offstage before appearing onstage to complete it.

14. Bacchus calls joyously to Ariadne, who mistakes him for Death coming to release her from her grief.

15. At the opening of the opera, the spirits of wine and beer sing about how they are man's friend, dispelling fatigue and worry.

*Given in its original Sicilian spelling; in some performances the song is sung in Italian instead.
**One point per extra credit answer.

7. ANSWERS

1. Rosa Ponselle.
2. Maria Callas.
3. Jan Peerce.
4. Emma Calve.
5. Nellie Melba.
6. Alma Gluck.
7. Louise Homer.
8. George London.
9. Richard Tauber.
10. Ernestine Schumann-Heink.
11. Charles Anthony.
12. Cristina Deutekom.
13. Marisa Galvany.
14. Victoria de los Angeles.
15. Alfredo Kraus.
16. Susanne Marsee.
17. Robert Merrill.
18. Gerald Souzay.
19. Richard van Allan.
20. Joyce Castle.

Extra Credit:

A. Franco Zeffirelli.
B. Lorenzo da Ponte.
C. Ruffo Titta.

8. ANSWERS*

In all cases, their libretti were written by their respective composers.

Extra Credit:

A. Colette.
B. Franco Zeffirelli.
C. Peter Pears.

*Ten points for the correct answer to the main question, two points per A, B, and C.

9. ANSWERS

1. Mohammed.
2. Silver Dollar.
3. Jerome.
4. Feodor.
5. Jemmy.

6. Catalina.
7. Gherardino.
8. Harry.
9. Max.
10. Willie.

Extra Credit:*

Charlotte, Sophie, Hans, Gretel, Karl, Clara, Max, and Fritz.

*One point per correct name in the extra credit section.

10. ANSWERS

1. g
2. b
3. h
4. o
5. k
6. m
7. l
8. o

9. e
10. a
11. d
12. n
13. i
14. j
15. f

Extra Credit:*

A. I. iii
    II. iv
    III. i
    IV. ii

B. V. viii
    VI. v
    VII. vi
    VIII. vii

*One point for each answer to A and B.

11. ANSWERS

1. Sophocles.
2. Euripides.
3. Tacitus.
4. Homer.
5. Virgil.
6. Euripides.
7. Ovid.
8. Euripides.
9. Ovid.
10. Sophocles.

Extra Credit:*

A. i. Midas.
    ii. A fly.
    iii. A laurel tree.
    iv. A spring.
B. Livy.
C. *The Frogs*, By Aristophanes.

*One point per answer to A and C, and two points for B.

12. ANSWERS

1. *Semele.*
2. *Vanessa.*
3. *Tosca.*
4. *Turandot.*
5. *Patience.*
6. *Manon.*
7. *Sweeney Todd.*
8. *Norma.*
9. *Faust.*
10. *Orphée aux Enfers.*
11. *The Gondoliers.*
12. *Das Rheingold.*
13. *Alessandro.*
14. *Cavalleria Rusticana.*
15. *La Muette de Portici.*

Extra Credit:*

Fist, nose, cheeks, bosom, eyes, tongue, foot, throat, face, hair, lip, breast, brow, and heart.

*One point per item named.

13. ANSWERS

1. *Paul Bunyan.*
2. *Albert Herring.*
3. *The Mighty Casey.*
4. *Ba-Ta-Clan.*
5. *The Mikado.*
6. *Sir John in Love.*
7. *Help! Help! The Globolinks!*
8. *Susannah.*
9. *A Midsummer Night's Dream.*
10. *The Tender Land.*
11. *The Bartered Bride.*
12. *Les Contes d'Hoffmann.*
13. *The Abduction of Figaro.*
14. *La Grand Duchesse de Gérolstein.*
15. *The Love for Three Oranges.*

Extra Credit:*

A. Corno di Bassetto.
B. Esteban Ria Nido (a literal Spanish translation of his name).

C.   I. *The Consul.*

II. *Die Frau ohne Schatten.*

III. *Ariadne auf Naxos.*

IV. *Suor Angelica.*

V. *Wozzeck.*

*Two points for A and B, one point for each answer to C.

14. ANSWERS

1. h	11. p
2. e	12. f
3. o	13. s
4. k	14. q
5. i	15. d
6. b	16. r
7. a	17. f
8. m	18. l
9. n	19. g
10. j	20. c

Extra Credit:*

A. Figaro in *Il Barbiere di Siviglia,* and Andrea Chenier in *Andrea Chénier.*

B. *La Traviata,* with New York City Opera.

C. *"Zweiter Knabe"* ("Second Boy") in *Die Zauberflöte.*

*Two points for B and C, one point each for the roles in A.

15. ANSWERS

1. j	9. l
2. f	10. b
3. l	11. n
4. a	12. m
5. g	13. e
6. o	14. k
7. d	15. h
8. c	

Extra Credit:

A. *Billy Budd* (his co-librettist was Eric Crozier).

B. W. H. Auden.

C. Gian Carlo Menotti.

16. ANSWERS

1. Thirty-six.
2. Eight (he's allowed seven free).
3. These are the men whose names are cried out by the women who look out their windows during the Act II melee.
4. Woglinde in *Das Rheingold.*
5. Alberich in *Das Rheingold.*
6. Mime in *Das Rheingold.*
7. *Der Fliegende Holländer.*
8. Nothung.
9. Holda, goddess of spring.
10. Alberich.
11. Grimhilde.
12. The dead warriors strapped to their backs were enemies.
13. His father, Gamuret.
14. The Southwind.
15. His back.

Extra Credit:*

A. h	G. j
B. d	H. l
C. i	I. k
D. g	J. e
E. b	K. f
F. a	L. c

*One point per answer.

17. ANSWERS

1. *Casanova.*	6. *Die Walküre.*
2. *Rigoletto.*	7. *Otello.*
3. *Les Troyens.*	8. *Peter Grimes.*
4. *Der Fliegende Holländer.*	9. *La Cenerentola.*
5. *Lucia di Lammermoor.*	10. *La Fanciulla del West.*

Extra Credit:

A. *L'Eclair* (The Lightning Bolt) by Halévy, composer of *La Juive.*
B. *Intermezzo* by Richard Strauss.
C. *Lodoletta* by Mascagni.

18. ANSWERS

1. *Falstaff.*
2. *Turandot* (unfinished).
3. *Carmen.*
4. *Les Contes d'Hoffmann* (unfinished).
5. *The Story of a Real Man.*
6. *Guillaume Tell.*
7. *The Emerald Isle* (unfinished).

8. *I Puritani.*
9. *Parsifal.*
10. *L'Africaine.*
11. *Death in Venice.*
12. *Die Zauberflöte.*
13. *Yolanta.*
14. *Capriccio.*
15. *Le Coq d'Or.*

Extra Credit:*

Don Pasquale, Maria di Rohan and, lastly, *Dom Sebastian* (all 1843).

*One point per extra credit title, two points for knowing which was the last work; also, one extra point for each correctly-guessed "unfinished" of the main section of the quiz.

19. ANSWERS*

The answers are given in this order: composer/lyricist

1. Rodgers/Hammerstein.
2. Bernstein/Sondheim.
3. G. Gershwin/I. Gershwin and Heyward.
4. Sondheim/Sondheim.
5. Lerner/Loewe.
6. Porter/Porter.
7. Kern/Hammerstein.
8. Rodgers/Hammerstein.
9. Bernstein/Wilbur, LaTouche & Sondheim.
10. Wright/Forrest.
11. Lerner/Loewe.
12. Wright/Forrest.
13. Adler/Ross.
14. Rodgers/Hammerstein.
15. Sondheim/Sondheim.

Extra Credit:

A. Lawrence A. and Mae Wien.
B. *Candide.*
C. Dorothy Parker.

*One point per composer or individual lyricist name in main body of the quiz (total possible: thirty-three points); two points per extra credit question.

20. ANSWERS

1. The Duke of Mantua.	6. Marguerite.
2. Edgardo.	7. Figaro.
3. Hoffmann.	8. Giorgio Germont.
4. Le Comte des Grieux.	9. Sarastro.
5. Elisabetta.	10. Roméo.

Extra Credit:*

The original singers, Giulia Grisi (Elvira), Giovanni-Battista Rubini (Arturo), and Antonio Tamburini and Luigi Lablanche (the two Walton brothers) became so famous for their roles that they were known thereafter as the *"Puritani* Quartet."

*One point per singer name, one point per role name.

21. ANSWERS

1. *Les Troyens.*
2. Teatro Amazonas (where Caruso is mistakenly believed to have performed—the closest he ever got was to visit the town in which it is located).
3. Deutsche Oper Berlin (Götz Friedrich directed).
4. Frankfurt Opera House.
5. Lyons.
6. Italy.
7. United States (Chicago).
8. Rotterdam, where the opera received its world premiere in 1980 by the Netherlands Opera.
9. Leonard Balada's *Christóbal Colón* (the tenor was José Carreras, who needed the time to recover from leukemia).

10. Vienna Volksoper.
11. Les Arts Florissants.
12. *Elisabetta di Siberia.*
13. Puccini.
14. Teatro Rossini, in Pesaro, Italy.
15. *Madama Butterfly.*

Extra Credit:*

A. I. d, e
    II. c
    III. a
    IV. d
    V. b
B. *Boris Godunov, Eugene Onegin, Pique Dame, War and Peace,* and *The Gambler.*
C. *Macbeth, La Bohème, La Cenerentola,* and *Simon Boccanegra.*

*One point for each correct letter answer to A, and for each opera title in B and C.

22. ANSWERS

1. Ruggero.
2. Amilcare.
3. Daniel.
4. Bedrich.
5. Riccardo.

6. Umberto.
7. Vincenzo.
8. Mikhail.
9. Gaetano.
10. Emmerich.

Extra Credit:

A. Jakob Liebmann Beer.
B. Elias Lévy.
C. Gioacchino.

23. ANSWERS

1. Adelina Patti.
2. *"Non più andrai"* from *Le Nozze di Figaro.*
3. "The Groves of Blarney" (better known as "The Last Rose of Summer").

4. "The Star-Spangled Banner."
5. *La Traviata.*
6. *"La blondina in gondoletta."*
7. *Orfeo ed Euridice ("Che farò senzo Euridice").*
8. *"Notte e giorno faticare"* from *Don Giovanni.*
9. *H.M.S. Pinafore.*
10. *"Ich grolle nicht."*

Extra Credit:*

A. Giuseppe Sarti's *Il Due Litiganti* and Martin y Soler's *Una Cosa Rara.*
B. "Hail to the school that floats the banner blue" is the song of New York City's Julia Richmond High School.
C. *Monsieur Choufleuri.*

*One point each for composers' names and opera titles in A, two points each for B and C.

24. ANSWERS

1. Naples.
2. Paris.
3. Plymouth.
4. Rome.
5. Seville.
6. Florence.
7. Stockholm.
8. Rome.
9. Prague.
10. Mainz.
11. Seville.
12. Vienna.
13. Verona.
14. Mantua.
15. Antwerp.

Extra Credit.:

A. Louisana.
B. South Carolina.
C. Tennessee.

25. ANSWERS

1. *Fidelio.*
2. *Il Barbiere di Siviglia.*
3. *Martha.*
4. *Ruddigore.*
5. *La Cenerentola.*
6. *Roberto Deveraux.*
7. *H.M.S. Pinafore.*
8. *The Gondoliers.*
9. *The Pirates of Penzance.*
10. *Zar und Zimmerman.*

Extra Credit:*

A. Busoni's *Arlecchio.*
B. Auber's *Fra Diavolo.*
C. *"La Prise de Troie"* and *"Les Troyens à Carthage."*

*Two points for A and B, one point per title in C.

26. ANSWERS

1. Chicago.	9. Vienna.
2. Vienna.	10. St. Petersburg.
3. Venice.	11. Prague.
4. Paris.	12. Monte Carlo.
5. New York.	13. Milan.
6. Venice.	14. Brussels.
7. Zurich.	15. Paris.
8. Paris.	

Extra Credit:

A. Contrary to popular belief, the opera was *Rigoletto.*
B. In NBC-TV's New York studio, from which the opera was broadcast live on Christmas Eve, 1951.
C. Venice.

27. ANSWERS

1. Chautauqa Institution.
2. Purchase, New York.
3. Peter Sellars.
4. The Santa Fe Opera.
5. New Jersey's Waterloo Festival.
6. The Santa Fe Opera.
7. The Mostly Mozart Festival.
8. Artpark, located in Lewiston, New York.
9. Charleston, South Carolina.
10. *The Ballad of Baby Doe,* which premiered in that city and concerns local history.
11. The company performs at Cooperstown, New York, which is also the home of the National Baseball Hall of Fame.
12. Virginia.

13. The New World Festival in Miami, Florida.
14. Lake George Opera Festival.
15. New York Grand Opera.

Extra Credit:*

A. *Orlando, Ariodante, Semele,* and *Alessandro.*
B. The U.S. premiere of *La Vera Storia,* plus *Falstaff, Elektra,* and *Tosca.*
C. *Don Giovanni, Le Nozze di Figaro,* and *Così Fan Tutte,* all staged by Peter Sellars.

*One point per correct opera title.

28. ANSWERS*

A.	7	c	I.	11	a	
B.	6	f	J.	8	n	
C.	1	j	K.	7	m	
D.	2	h	L.	4	g	
E.	10	b	M.	9	k	
F.	3	e	N.	5	d	
G.	2	1	O.	9	i	
H.	11	c				

*One point for each correct number or lowercase letter.

29. ANSWERS

1. Jessye Norman.
2. Jerry Hadley.
3. Tito Gobbi.
4. Eric Idle.
5. Bonaventura Bottone.
6. Alain Vanzo.
7. *Manon.*
8. *West Side Story.*
9. New Jersey's Paper Mill Playhouse.
10. Samuel Ramey was Don Giovanni, Ferruccio Furlanetto was Leporello.
11. Carol Burnett.
12. Vincent Price.
13. Francisco Araiza.
14. Rockwell Blake.
15. 1986.

Extra Credit:*

A. The opera was *La Bohème;* the singers/roles as follows:
Allan Monk: Schaunard in both performances.
Italo Tajo: Benoit in both performances, plus Alcindoro in 1982.
Dale Caldwell: Parpignol.
Renata Scotto: Mimi in 1977, Musetta in 1982.
B. Monserrat Caballé, Marilyn Horne, Francisco Araiza, Ruggero Raimondi, and Samuel Ramey.
C. *Les Mamelles de Tirésias, Arabella, La Bohème, Die Zauberflöte* and *Samson et Dalila.*

*One point per opera, singer, and role (role points total six).

30. ANSWERS

1. Rimsky-Korsakov.		6. Verdi.
2. Gounod.		7. Sullivan.
3. Tchaikovsky.		8. Herbert.
4. Prokofiev.		9. Tauber.
5. Boito.		10. Debussy.

Extra Credit:*

1. *Boris Godunov.*
2. *Le Médecin Malgré Lui.*
3. *Carmen,* said to have influenced his own *Pique Dame.*
4. *The Love for Three Oranges,* which premiered in America in French.
5. Verdi's *Falstaff* and *Otello.*
6. *King Lear* (whose librettist was to have been Boito).
7. *Ivanhoe,* which ran for 160 performances.
8. Cello.
9. Lehár.
10. "The Fall of the House of Usher."

*One point per answer.

31. ANSWERS

1. *Giulio Cesare.*
2. September 27, 1988.
3. Jeffrey Gall and Derek Lee Ragin.
4. *A Midsummer Night's Dream;* the role is Oberon.
5. Albert Deller.
6. Paul Esswood.
7. The Voice of Apollo.
8. James Bowman.
9. *Pacific Overtures.*
10. Endymion.

Extra Credit:*

A. Xerxes was sung by a mezzo and Arsamene by a countertenor.
B. Drew Minter.
C. La Gran Scena Opera Co.

*One point for each answer to A, two points each for B and C.

32. ANSWERS

1. DuBose Heyward's *Porgy.*
2. Todd Duncan.
3. Anne Brown.
4. Sidney Poitier.
5. Dorothy Dandridge.
6. The Gershwin estate forbids any other casting.*
7. It is an account of the 1955 Russian tour of the opera, which was performed in English without any available Russian libretto to aid its audiences' understanding!
8. Marian Anderson.
9. Ulrica.
10. Robert McFerrin.
11. Amonasro.
12. Langston Hughes.
13. Henry Davis.
14. Reri Grist.
15. Consuelo (the soloist in "Somewhere").

Extra Credit:**

A. Colline *La Bohème.*
B. Amneris *Aïda.*
C. Elisabeth *Tannhäuser.*
D. Micaëla *Carmen.*
E. Lampanaio *Manon Lescaut.*
F. Erisbe *Ormindo.*

*A notable exception: The New Zealand opera was permitted to employ Maori singers in their *Porgy and Bess.*
**Score one point for each correct answer.

33. ANSWERS

1. *The Crucible.*
2. *Lost in the Stars.*
3. South Africa.
4. *The Most Important Man.*
5. *La Forza del Destino* (Don Alvaro).
6. *The Emperor Jones.*
7. Eugene O'Neill.
8. Lawrence Tibbett.
9. Texarkana, Texas.
10. *Treemonisha.*
11. Her adopted mother, Monisha, found her beneath a tree.
12. Bags of luck.
13. *Satyagraha.*
14. Auber's *Manon Lescaut.*
15. Gomes's *Lo Schiavo.*

Extra Credit:

A. The Amato Opera.
B. Paul Robeson.
C. *A Guest of Honor.*

34. ANSWERS

1. *The Passion of Jonathan Wade.*
2. South Carolina.
3. Lucas Wardlaw.
4. *Four Saints in Three Acts.*
5. Spain.
6. Adah le Clerq.
7. Julie.
8. Thea Musgrave. The opera is *Harriet: A Woman Called Moses.*
9. *Troubled Island.*
10. William Grant Still.
11. Jean Jacques Dessalines.
12. Anthony Davis.
13. His cousin, Thulani Davis.
14. Ben Holt.
15. Kathleen Battle.

Extra Credit:

A. Thomas Bowers.
B. Sissieretta Jones.
C. Caterina Jarlboro.

35. ANSWERS

1. Portsmouth, England.
2. The first person he sees when he lands safely. Unfortunately, this turns out to be his own son.
3. The *Seagull.*
4. Cape Finisterre, owned by the French.
5. The Lake of the Four Cantons.
6. *Rinaldo.*
7. The *Santa Rosalia.*
8. Silvano.
9. Ligunia.
10. *Hecate.*
11. Galicia.
12. The *Cotton Blossom.*
13. Sandwyk.
14. Captain Corcoran.
15. *La Gioconda.*

Extra Credit:

A. Lord Nelson's *H.M.S. Victory.*
B. *H.M.S. Semaphore.* He needed something to rhyme with "more."
C. Cunard and P & O.

36. ANSWERS

1. Cimarosa.
2. Auber.
3. Liszt.
4. Catalani.
5. Massenet.
6. Donizetti.
7. Paderewski.
8. Gounod.
9. Verdi.
10. Borodin.
11. Ravel.
12. Meyerbeer.
13. Rossini.
14. Respighi.
15. Menotti.

Extra Credit:*

A. Boieldieu's *La Dame Blanche,* Donizetti's *Lucrezia Borgia,* and Nicolai's *The Merry Wives of Windsor.*
B. Bizet's *Les Pêcheurs de Perles.*
C. *Diana of Salange.*

*Score one point for each opera in question A, and two points each for the answers to B and C.

37. ANSWERS

1. 1935.
2. Anne Kaskas and Arthur Carron.
3. Rockwell Blake.
4. $20,000.
5. All have been winners of the Naumberg Competition.
6. *The Consul.*
7. Gian Carlo Menotti, for *The Consul* and *The Saint of Bleecker Street.*
8. *Giants of the Earth.*
9. *The Crucible.*
10. Leontyne Price.

Extra Credit:

A. Each pair was chosen as finalists of Met Auditions in the same year.
B. William Schuman.
C. *Docteur Miracle.* He shared the first prize with Alexandre-Charles Lecocq.

38. ANSWERS

1. h	9. l
2. j	10. c
3. f	11. e
4. k	12. b
5. a	13. i
6. k	14. g
7. d	15. i
8. e	

Extra Credit:

A. Coca-Cola.
B. *La Périchole.*
C. *La Grande Duchesse de Gérolstein.*

39. ANSWERS

1. m	9. n
2. a	10. j
3. f	11. e
4. j	12. d
5. c	13. l
6. k	14. l
7. b	15. g
8. h	

Extra Credit:

A. Don Giovanni d'Aragona.
B. *The Libertine.*
C. He was a tenor in its chorus.

40. ANSWERS

1. France.	6. Italy.
2. France.	7. France.
3. Switzerland.	8. England.
4. France.	9. United States.
5. Franc.	10. France.

Extra Credit:

A. This was the year that the composer became a British citizen.
B. United States.
C. United States.

41. ANSWERS

1. f	6. h
2. e	7. d
3. h	8. g
4. e	9. a
5. b	10. c

Extra Credit:

A. *I Due Foscari.*
B. Weber began it, Mahler finished it.
C. Four.

42. ANSWERS

1. *The Temple of Minerva,* staged in 1781.
2. Francis Hopkinson.
3. Rossini's *Il Barbiere di Siviglia* (it was done in English nine years earlier).
4. James Mapleson.
5. Bristow's *Rip Van Winkle.*
6. Fry's *Leonora.*
7. New Orleans.
8. P. T. Barnum.
9. Howard Hanson.
10. *Merry Mount.*

Extra Credit:

A. Annie Louise Cary, who sang Ortrud in 1877.
B. Brooklyn, New York (Amina, in 1866, when she was fourteen).
C. *Hänsel und Gretel.*

43. ANSWERS

1. Poker.
2. Faro.
3. Faro.
4. Sid.
5. Three aces and a pair.
6. Seven.
7. Four (Mercedes has three read).
8. The ghost of the Countess.
9. Dominoes.
10. His horses and armor.
11. Robert, sent on a wild goose chase, has not shown up for the match; the Prince wins by default.
12. Skat.
13. Zara.
14. 100 zecchini.
15. Routellenberg.

Extra Credit:

A. Three shillings (or, in modern terms, thirty-six pence).
B. *La Fanciulla del West.*
C. Poussette bets on Guillot, Javotte on the Chevalier des Grieux

44. ANSWERS

1. f	6. a
2. d and g	7. j
3. g and h	8. e
4. b	9. c
5. b	10. i

Extra Credit:

A. Elisabeth Billington.
B. Louis XVI.
C. *The Gondoliers* . . . and she *was* amused.

45. ANSWERS

1. i	9. e
2. k	10. g
3. a	11. n
4. o	12. h
5. j	13. l
6. b	14. d
7. m	15. f
8. c	

Extra Credit:

A. Nino Rota.
B. Offenbach's *Barkouf.*
C. *L'Oiseau Bleu,* composed by Albert Wolff.

46. ANSWERS

1. b	6. d
2. i	7. j
3. e	8. c
4. a	9. g
5. h	10. f

Extra Credit:

A. Schoenberg's *Erwartung.*
B. Smetana.
C. *From the House of the Dead.*

47. ANSWERS

1. Eight.
2. Lorin Maazel.
3. José van Dam.
4. James Levine.
5. *And the Ship Sails On.*
6. *Fitzcarraldo.*
7. Kathryn Harrold.
8. Francesco Rosi.

  9. Three hundred minutes (five hours).
10. *Moonstruck.*
11. *Apocalypse Now.*
12. *The Witches of Eastwick.*
13. *Distant Harmony.*
14. *The Mikado.*
15. *Madama Butterfly* (lent by the San Francisco Opera; the singers, however, were New York City Opera artists).

Extra Credit:*

Bill Bryden, Nicolas Roeg, Charles Sturridge, Jean-Luc Godard, Julien Temple, Bruce Beresford, Robert Altman, Franc Roddam, Ken Russell, and Derek Jarman.

*Score one point apiece.

48. ANSWERS

  1. *Metropolitan.*
  2. *San Francisco.*
  3. *Naughty Marietta.*
  4. *The Great Victor Herbert.*
  5. *The Search.*
  6. *The Great Waltz* (about Johann Strauss II).
  7. Miliza Korjus.
  8. *Because You're Mine.*
  9. *The Big Broadcast of 1938.*
10. *It's a Date.*
11. *100 Men and a Girl.*
12. He played both Tonio and Silvio.
13. *I Dream Too Much.*
14. *Song O' My Heart.*
15. Gertrude Lawrence.

Extra Credit:*

A. Bruce Dargavel.
B. Monica Sinclair.
C. Dorothy Bond.
D. Margherita Grandi.
E. Hoffmann was both acted and sung by Robert Rounseville.
F. Antonia was both acted and sung by Ann Ayars.

*Score one point apiece.

49. ANSWERS

1. Seven.
2. Two months.
3. Five.
4. One thousand.
5. One year.
6. One year.
7. Seven years.
8. Twenty-seven years.
9. Twenty-five years.
10. One hundred.
11. Fourteen weeks.
12. Thirty.
13. Thirty-two.
14. Three.
15. *The Last Savage.*

Extra Credit:

A. *L'Enfant et les Sortilèges.*
B. The Greek letter pi (π).
C. Major-General Stanley.

50. ANSWERS

1. *Capriccio.*
2. *Daphne* and *Ariadne auf Naxos.*
3. *Louise.*
4. Boleslao Lazuski.
5. Stolz's *Zwei Herzen im Dreivierteltakt* (Two Hearts in Three-Quarter Time).
6. *The Man Who Mistook His Wife for a Hat.*
7. *Help! Help! The Globolinks!*
8. *The Consul.*
9. Mabel Mercer.
10. Caffariello.
11. *The Last Savage.*

12. *The Little Sweep.*
13. *Regina.*
14. *The Last Savage.*
15. *The Aspern Papers.*

Extra Credit:

A. *Il Viaggio a Reims.*
B. Fiando Fiorinelli.
C. Alcazar.

51. ANSWERS

1. k	7. l
2. e	8. c
3. a	9. f
4. h	10. d
5. j	11. g
6. b	12. i

Extra Credit:

A. Lauritz Melchior and Beniamino Gigli, both born March 20, 1890.
B. Mirella Freni (born 2/27/35) and Luciano Pavarotti (born 10/12/35).
C Eugene and Herbert Perry.

52. ANSWERS

1. The Coliseum, home of the English National Opera.
2. Sadler's Wells Opera.
3. All operas performed by the English National Opera are sung in English (the Royal Opera does employ English surtitles to aid in audience understanding of their works).
4. Glyndebourne.
5. John Christie.
6. Sir Rudolf Bing.
7. Three, successively built in the same vicinity after each previous theater burned down. The present theater opened in 1858.
8. 1968.

9. *Ivanhoe.*
10. *The Siege of Rhodes,* which premiered in 1656. It was written by five composers, and featured in its cast the first woman to appear on public stage in England.
11. The Earl of Harewood.
12. John Mauceri.
13. Opera North.
14. The Welsh National Opera.
15. *Aïda.*

Extra Credit:*

A. The festival was founded by frequent collaborators Benjamin Britten, Peter Pears, and Eric Crozier. Aldeburgh was Britten's hometown.
B. The Beecham Opera Company, which was founded in 1910 and folded in 1919.
C. Walpole.

*One point for each founder and final question in A, two points each for the answers to B and C.

53. ANSWERS

1. i	9. a
2. g	10. c
3. b	11. d
4. f	12. e
5. j	13. h
6. d	14. e
7. i	15. k
8. i	

Extra Credit:*

A. Le Bal Musard, Frascati's, Cadet's, Pré Catelan, and Bullier's.
B. *Chérubin.*
C. The Garter Inn, in *Falstaff.*

*Score 1 point for each correct name in A, and two points each for answers to B and C.

54. ANSWERS

1. A ring.
2. 100 yen.
3. Two florins.
4. 50,000 marks.
5. One zecchin.
6. $1.50.
7. $4.
8. Quattro droppie.

9. 10,000 marks.
10. 100 scudi.
11. 30,000 livres.
12. The title to Gaunersdorf.
13. A ring.
14. 50 ducats.
15. Alice, in *Falstaff.*

Extra Credit:

A. Andrew Borden in *Lizzie Borden.*
B. *Porgy and Bess* (the dead man is Robbins).
C. Leo Fall.

55. ANSWERS

1. d
2. a
3. f
4. b
5. c

6. h
7. e
8. d
9. i
10. g

Extra Credit:

A. *Zaza.*
B. *Capriccio.*
C. *Summer and Smoke.*

56. ANSWERS

1. n
2. o
3. e
4. h
5. m
6. j
7. f
8. l

9. d
10. b
11. i
12. b
13. k
14. c
15. a

Extra Credit:

A. Barber.
B. Britten.
C. Bernstein.

57. ANSWERS

1. Eighty-six
2. Eighty-five
3. Ninety-five
4. Eighty-one
5. Eighty-one

6. Ninety-three
7. Eighty-five
8. Eighty-eight
9. Eighty-eight
10. Eighty-one

Extra Credit:

A. Eighty-four.
B. *New Year.*
C. Manuel Rosenthal.

58. ANSWERS

1. Lily Holmes.
2. *Manon Lescaut.*
3. The Countess's nightcap.
4. Hippolyte.
5. Eboli, in *Don Carlo.*
6. Otello throws it down when Desdemona tries to bandage his forehead with it, and then Emilia takes it.
7. *Don Rodrigo.*
8. Florinda.
9. *Louise.*
10. *The Last Savage.*
11. Lizzie, in *Lizzie Borden.*
12. An antique cross pendant with a secret compartment.
13. *Gloriana.*
14. A necklace of thirty pearls.
15. *L'Etoile.*

Extra Credit:

A. *L'Assedio di Corinto* (at La Scala).
B. Linda Roark-Strummer.
C. *Ariadne auf Naxos,* in keeping with the opera's first half being a "rehearsal."

59. ANSWERS

1. *The Consul*—as the Secretary flips through her files looking for the name "Sorel."
2. The other women being deported to America, in Puccini's *Manon Lescaut.*
3. Mignon.
4. Nelly.
5. Gaetano.
6. Pierre.
7. Octavian.
8. Quinquin.
9. Pierce.
10. Edward Fairfax Vere.
11. Tannhauser.
12. Carlo.
13. Barbara.
14. Steve.
15. Carlotto.

Extra Credit:*

A. Welko, Djura, and Jankel.
B. Sempronio and Tizia, respectively.
C. Ned, Will, Tom, and Isaac.

*Score one point for each correct name.

60. ANSWERS

1. April 10, 1900.
2. February 21, 1965.
3. December 1, 1299.
4. February 29.
5. 1940.
6. 1797.
7. 1860.
8. December 26, 1774.

9. April 1899.
10. June 1794.
11. 1647.
12. April 17, 1860.
13. 1414.
14. 452 A.D.
15. 1900.

Extra Credit:

A. The Year of the Tiger, in which the opera is set.
B. December 24, 1856.
C. *Monsieur Choufleuri Restera Chez Lui le 24 Janvier 1833.*

61. ANSWERS

1. Mariandel.
2. Sister Colette.
3. Leukippos.
4. *Les Mamelles de Tirésias.*
5. 40,049.
6. Vasili, a hussar.
7. His employer catches him shaving.
8. *Le Convenienze Teatrali* (sometimes performed as the revised and expanded *Le Convenienze ed Inconvenienze Teatrali,* in which the "woman" appears in an opera-within-the-opera as a man).
9. Antonio.
10. *Casanova.*
11. *Mesdames de la Halle.*
12. Maximilian.
13. Creonte.
14. Bardolph.
15. Flute.

Extra Credit:

A. Jay Reise's *Rasputin.*
B. Marcello.
C. Linfea.

62. ANSWERS

1. A donkey.
2. A lion.
3. The Animal Tamer in *Lulu.*
4. *Of Mice and Men.*
5. *Der Rosenkavalier.*
6. A donkey.
7. Queenie.
8. Marcellina.
9. *La Wally.*
10. *Der Junge Lord.*
11. Sir Arthur Sullivan.
12. A bull.
13. Daniel Webster.
14. He feeds Daniel buckshot to weigh him down.
15. *Candide.*

Extra Credit:

A. *Paul Bunyan.*
B. *Gloriana.*
C. Nero.

63. ANSWERS

Each opera has no overture.

Extra Credit:

A. *Aureliano in Palmira.*
B. *The Bartered Bride.*
C. *Aïda.*

*Ten points for the correct answer to the main question, two points per extra credit answer.

64. ANSWERS

1. f	9. b
2. c, g	10. l
3. f	11. m
4. h	12. i
5. j	13. d, j
6. d	14. e
7. k	15. h
8. a	

Extra Credit:

A. *La Rondine.*
B. *Four Saints in Three Acts.*
C. Henry Price, who sang the role of St. Chavez.

65. ANSWERS

1. Midnight.	9. Noon.
2. 7 A.M.	10. Midnight.
3. 11 P.M.	11. Noon.
4. Midnight.	12. 9 A.M.
5. Midnight.	13. 11 A.M.
6. 10 P.M.	14. Midnight.
7. 5 A.M.	15. 7 P.M.
8. 8:15 P.M.	

Extra Credit:

A. Gonzalve and Don Inigo.
B. 7 A.M. to 11 P.M.
C. 2 P.M. to 3 P.M.

*Score one point for each name in A, and two points each for B and C.

66. ANSWERS

1. j	9. n
2. e	10. m
3. g	11. h
4. k	12. p
5. a	13. o
6. b	14. d
7. c	15. f, i
8. l	

Extra Credit:

A. *"Parmi veder le lagrime."*
B. Serena.
C. *Treemonisha.*

67. ANSWERS

1. An eagle.	9. A parrot.
2. A white dove.	10. Her Great Auk.
3. A jaybird.	11. Doves.
4. *Noye's Fludde.*	12. *Sweeney Todd.*
5. A turtledove.	13. The *Tom-Tit.*
6. *La Belle Hélène.*	14. The Astrologer.
7. *H.M.S. Pinafore.*	15. *The Yeomen of the Guard.*
8. *Roméo et Juliette.*	

Extra Credit:

A. *Lizzie Borden.*
B. *Don Rodrigo.*
C. *The Cunning Little Vixen.*

68. ANSWERS

1. He is wounded by Octavian's sword.
2. To blow a foreign body out of his eye.
3. Mustafa.
4. Paisiello's *Il Barbiere di Siviglia.*
5. *Le Postillon de Longjumeau.*

6. *La Fille du Tambour-Major.*
7. The Offenbach pastiche *Christopher Columbus.*
8. Cholera.
9. Mandryka, after a run-in with a bear.
10. Jakey in *Porgy and Bess.*
11. Cholrea.
12. Pirelli.
13. Syphilis.
14. Arsenic.
15. Women of her station don't *need* smelling salts.

Extra Credit:

A. Shirley MacLaine.
B. A veterinarian.
C. *Le Médecin Malgré Lui.*

69. ANSWERS

1. m	9. b
2. i	10. f
3. e	11. h
4. a, g	12. o
5. p	13. k
6. d	14. l
7. j	15. n
8. c	

Extra Credit:*

A. Fred Plotkin, who served a number of years as their performance manager.
B. Jerome Hines.
C. *Bubbles: A Self Portrait.*
   Bubbles: An Encore.
   Beverly: An Autobiography.

*Two points each for A and B, one point for each answer to C.

70. ANSWERS

1. h	6. b
2. c	7. a
3. a	8. i
4. f	9. e
5. g	10. d

Extra Credit:*

A. Leonard Bernstein.
B. *Carmen, Madama Butterfly, Die Zauberflöte,* and *Der Fliegende Holländer.*
C. *Giant's Bread* was the title, Agatha Christie the real author.

*Two points each for A and C, and one point for each title in B.

71. ANSWERS

1. d	9. a
2. i	10. b
3. m	11. o
4. j	12. g
5. l	13. c
6. n	14. h
7. f	15. e
8. k	

Extra Credit:

A. *Louise.*
B. *La Pomme d'Api.*
C. *Zaza.*

72. ANSWERS

1. A telephone.
2. *Les Mamelles de Tirésias.*
3. *The Cradle Will Rock.*
4. A jukebox (the aria really *was* a pop song of the fifties, sung by Mario Lanza).

5. *The Consul.*
6. *Paul Bunyon.*
7. *The Story of a Real Man.*
8. *The Last Savage.*
9. *Four Saints in Three Acts.*
10. *Gallantry.*

Extra Credit:

A. Glass's *Einstein on the Beach.*
B. *La Voyage de la Lune.*
C. *Trouble in Tahiti.*

73. ANSWERS

1. The Houston Grand Opera.
2. Ardis Krainik.
3. The Skylight Comic Opera of Milwaukee.
4. Speight Jenkins.
5. George London.
6. *Aïda.*
7. The Opera Company of Philadelphia.
8. Nikolaus Lehnhoff.
9. Donald Pippin.
10. Ginastera's *Beatrix Cenci.*
11. The St. Paul Opera Association.
12. The Houston Grand Opera.
13. A movie house.
14. Francois Rochaix.
15. The San Diego Opera.

Extra Credit:

A. Dallas (by the Dallas Opera) and Evanston, Illinois (by Northwestern University).
B. Minnesota Opera Theater.
C. *Idomeneo.*

74. ANSWERS

1. f	9. k
2. d	10. e
3. a	11. o
4. n	12. g
5. b	13. i
6. j	14. l
7. m	15. h
8. c	

Extra Credit:

A. Ambassador to London.

B. The three princesses of the oranges, in *The Love for Three Oranges.*

C. Ulric, Prince of Tieffenburg.

75. ANSWERS

1. *La Cenerentola* (Don Magnifico's vision of what meal he will have when a daughter is married to the prince).
2. *The Sorcerer* (the banquet where the philtre is administered).
3. *La Jolie Fille de Perth* (the proposed wedding feast).
4. *Paul Bunyan* (Christmas dinner).
5. *Falstaff* (Falstaff's meal).
6. *Manon* (the offerings at the inn, in Act I).
7. *Hänsel und Gretel* (what Father brings home for supper).
8. *Hänsel und Gretel* (what the Witch promises the children).
9. *Le Jongleur de Notre-Dame* (the meal Boniface prepares).
10. *Suor Angelica* (the foods supporters have brought to the convent).
11. *La Bohème* (Christmas dinner at the cafe).
12. *Albert Herring* (the May Day feast as described by the children).
13. *Albert Herring* (the May Day feast as recalled by Albert).

Extra Credit:

A. *Paul Bunyan.*
B. *Le Docteur Miracle.*
C. *L'Etoile.*

76. ANSWERS

1. k	9. n
2. a	10. e
3. h	11. j
4. m	12. l
5. b	13. i
6. g	14. f
7. l	15. o
8. d	

Extra Credit:*

A. Honan, Kiu, and Tsiang.
B. *La Gioconda.*
C. Puccini's Manon Lescaut, when she's on the verge of being deported there.

*One point each for the answers to A, two points each for B and C.

77. ANSWERS

1. A blue handkerchief.
2. Queen Isabella.
3. Ten.
4. Statues of the twelve Apostles.
5. A donkey skin.
6. A gold chain.
7. Madame Armfeldt.
8. The Eusinian Sea.
9. Harry Easter in *Street Scene,* wooing Rose.
10. A bow and arrows.
11. He ordered the streets of Verona to be covered thickly with salt.
12. A ruby clasp.

13. Antonio, her foster father.
14. A handerchief, accompanied by a card saying it was from her and the man Alma loved.
15. A bracelet.

Extra Credit:*

A. Flowers, perfume, and lace, respectively.
B. Salome (Herod is the man doing the offering).
C. Lady Billows gives him a purse of 25 sovereigns, the Mayor presents Albert with a savings passbook listing a balance of five pounds, and Miss Wordsworth's school sends him Foxes' *Book of Martyrs*—in two volumes, illustrated, inscribed, and dated!

*One point for each answer to A and C, two points for B.

78. ANSWERS

1. Erich Kleiber.
2. Jean Fournet.
3. Riccardo Muti.
4. Antonio de Almeida.
5. Thomas Fulton.
6. Giuseppe Sinopoli.
7. Sir Georg Solti.
8. Judith Somogi.
9. Joan Dornemann.
10. The Met's *Aïda.*
11. Alessandro Siciliani.
12. Ileana Cotrubas.
13. Giuseppe Sinopoli.
14. Lorin Maazel.
15. Sergiu Comissiona.

Extra Credit:

A. Sarah Caldwell.
B. Julius Rudel.
C. Twenty-eight.

79. ANSWERS

1. Mulberry.
2. A red poppy.
3. Laurel.
4. A lilac bush.
5. Green orchids.
6. *La Jolie Fille de Perth.*
7. Orchids.
8. Gillyflowers.
9. Roses.
10. A datura.
11. Sage.
12. Willow.
13. Balsam.
14. Violets.
15. Edelweiss.

Extra Credit:

A. A thousand-year-old oak branch.
B. The Blue Flower.
C. It has been scented with oil of roses.

80. ANSWERS

1. Aunt Eth.
2. Ocunama.
3. McKinley.
4. Nina Micheltorena.
5. William Spode.
6. David.
7. Bianca.
8. Radbod.
9. Anna Viola.
10. Tyrone.
11. Bossuet.
12. Idia Legray.
13. The Prince of Conti.
14. Mitzi Mayer.
15. Charlotte Marie Adelaide von Zarkinow.

Extra Credit:*

A. Leonore, Gretchen, and Fausta, respectively.
B. Zerbinetta's old loves.
C. *Patience.*

*One point each for answers to A, two points each for B and C.

81. ANSWERS

1. La Scala, in 1969.
2. *Madama Butterfly* at the Met.
3. Peter Sellars.
4. *La Favorita,* at the Teatro La Fenice.
5. The Opera Theatre of St. Louis (the opera was *Così Fan Tutte*).
6. Sir Peter Hall.
7. Sarah Caldwell.
8. A 1986 *Carmen* for the Teatro San Carlo.
9. *Faust,* in 1990.
10. Graziella Sciutti.
11. Jean-Pierre Ponnelle.
12. *Carmen* at the Hamburg State Opera.
13. Göran Järvefelt.
14. Peter Brook.
15. Tito Capobianco.

Extra Credit:

A. Jonathan Miller.
B. Lotfollah ("Lotfi") Mansouri.
C. Frank Corsaro.

82. ANSWERS

1. The Houston Grand Opera.
2. Cris Groenendaal.
3. Joaquin Romaguera.
4. Timothy Nolen.
5. *A Little Night Music.*
6. Jonathan Tunick.
7. Paul Gemignani.
8. The score is written in, or in variations on, three-quarter time.
9. Mahler.
10. *The Bartered Bride.*
11. Erie Mills.
12. Licia Albanese.
13. English National Opera.
14. "A Stephen Sondheim Evening," recorded at Sotheby's 3/3/83 (the singer was Angela Lansbury).
15. The same as above, in the final selection "Old Friends" (from *Merrily We Roll Along),* which he began singing alone, and which became an ensemble by the entire cast.

Extra Credit:*

A. Mr. Lindquist, Mrs. Nordstrom, Mrs. Anderssen, Mr. Erlanson, and Mrs. Segstrom.
B. Oxford University.
C. Daniel O'Higgins.

*One point for each name in A, two points each for B and C.

83. ANSWERS

1. i	9. n
2. d	10. a
3. g	11. c
4. f	12. h
5. l	13. e
6. m	14. j
7. b	15. k
8. o	

Extra Credit:

A. The Hildebrands.
B. Lulu.
C. *Andrea Chénier.*

84. ANSWERS

1. *Il Mondo della Luna.*
2. Orff's *Der Mond.*
3. St. Peter.
4. Doris Lessing.
5. Philip Glass.
6. Peter Russell.
7. *Minutes Till Midnight.*
8. *New Yorker* science writer Daniel Lang.
9. *The Excursions of Mr. Brouček.*
10. *The Bride from Pluto.*
11. *La Voyage dans la Lune.*
12. *Help! Help! The Globolinks!*
13. Tonal music.
14. Paul Lincke.
15. In a balloon.

Extra Credit:

A. Pooh-Bah.
B. The alcoholic beverage shared by Dick and Mae.
C. *Aniara,* penned by Swedish composer Karl-Birger Blomdahl (this 1959 opera concerns passengers on a doomed spaceship).

85. ANSWERS

1. g	6. c
2. d	7. g
3. b	8. e
4. h	9. i, j
5. a	10. f

Extra Credit:

A. Sister Angela.
B. Fourteen.
C. The Sons and Daughters of Repent Ye Saith the Lord.

86. ANSWERS

1. June Anderson.	9. Ashley Putnam.
2. Ann Murray.	10. Marilyn Mims.
3. Arthur Davies.	11. Plácido Domingo.
4. William Guthrie.	12. Paul Plishka.
5. Hildegard Behrens.	13. *La Bohème.*
6. Aprile Millo.	14. Peter Hofmann.
7. Beverly Evans.	15. Stanford Olsen.
8. Eva Marton.	

Extra Credit:*

A. Giuseppe Patané and Eugene Kohn.
B. Neil Shicoff, Neil Rosenshein, and Neil Wilson.
C. When Neil Shicoff lost his voice early in the show, William Lewis—also indisposed vocally—mimed Hoffmann onstage while Kenneth Riegel sang the role from the orchestra pit.

*One point for each name.

87. ANSWERS

1. j	9. k
2. g	10. c
3. a	11. h
4. b	12. m
5. i	13. f
6. l	14. d
7. n	15. e
8. a	

Extra Credit:

A. *Sappho.*
B. Valzacchi.
C. *L'Enfant et les Sortilèges.*

88. ANSWERS

1. *Lakmé.*
2. *Le Jongleur de Notre-Dame.*
3. *Manon.*
4. *Louise.*
5. Dr. Coppelius, in *Les Contes d'Hoffmann.*
7. *La Bohème.*
8. *Porgy and Bess.*
9. *Street Scene.*
10. *Sweeney Todd.*

Extra Credit:

A. *The Rake's Progress.*
B. *La Forza del Destino.*
C. Ibert's *Angélique.*

89. ANSWERS

1. Berlioz.
2. Gounod.
3. Mozart.
4. Sullivan.
5. R. Strauss.
6. Haydn.
7. Schoenberg.
8. Wagner.

9. Puccini.
10. R. Strauss.
11. Gluck.
12. Offenbach.
13. Verdi.
14. Monteverdi.
15. Handel.

Extra Credit:*

1. Ravel.
2. Bizet.
3. Dvorak.
4. Stravinsky.
5. Henze.
6. E.T.A. Hoffmann.
7. R. Strauss.
8. Berlioz.

9. Shostakovich.
10. Tchaikovsky.
11. Handel.
12. Rossini.
13. Bizet.
14. Stravinsky.
15. Beethoven.

*One point each.

90. ANSWERS

1. *The Rake's Progress.*
2. *Maria Stuarda.*
3. *Porgy and Bess.*
4. *Dido and Aeneas.*
5. *Rienzi.*
6. *Les Huguenots.*
7. *Salome.*
8. *La Favorita.*

9. *Guillaume Tell.*
10. *Der Rosenkavalier.*
11. *Götterdämmerung.*
12. *Ernani.*
13. *Don Giovanni* and *Le Nozze di Figaro.*
14. *Pelléas and Mélisande.*
15. *Tristan und Isolde.*

Extra Credit:*

1. Britten.
2. Donizetti himself after its premiere.
3. Thomson.
4. Holst.
5. Sullivan.
6. Schumann.
7. Saint-Saëns.

8. Schumann.
9. Donizetti.
10. Stravinsky.
11. Fauré.
12. Gounod.
13. Beethoven.
14. Fauré.
15. Berlioz.

*One point each.

91. ANSWERS

1. d
2. a
3. g
4. h
5. i

6. b
7. d
8. f
9. c
10. e

Extra Credit:*

A. Dame Joan Sutherland.
B. Sir William, Little Billy, and Rudi.
C. Maurice Sendak.

*Two points each for A and C, one point for each answer to B.

92. ANSWERS

1. Soprano Alwina Valleria, who sang Leonora *Il Trovatore* during their first season.
2. Mrs. August Belmont.
3. J. P. Morgan.
4. *Hänsel und Gretel,* on 12/25/31.
5. *Il Trovatore.*
6. *Così Fan Tutte.*
7. *Phoebus and Pan.*

8. 1897–1898, cancelled with the death of general manager Henry Abbey. The Met's 1892–1893 had also been cancelled, as the result of a fire that had nearly destroyed the house.
9. *Samson et Dalila.*
10. 1/13/10—*Cavalleria Rusticana/Pagliacci.*
11. General Manager Giulio Gatti-Casazzo.
12. George Cehanovsky.
13. "Grand Operatic Surprise Party."
14. Rosina Galli, wife of Giulio Gatti-Casazzo.
15. 10/22/83.

Extra Credit:*

A. *Orfeo ed Euridice* (1936), *Le Coq d'Or* (1937) and *The Rake's Progress* (1953).
B. *Peter Ibbetson* by Deems Taylor; it was preceded in the afternoon by *Hänsel und Gretel.*
C. 1883–1884 was Italian, 1884–1885 was German.

*One point for each correct answer (total seven points).

93. ANSWERS

1. *Rinaldo.*
2. Flip City.
3. *Faust,* on 3/10/90.
4. Rise Stevens.
5. *Carmen.*
6. *Madama Butterfly,* shelved with the bombing of Pearl Harbor.
7. James Levine.
8. Goeran Gentele.
9. *Otello,* on 11/29/48.
10. Avery Fisher Hall, then known as Philharmonic Hall (the program consisted of Falla's *El Amor Brujo* and *Atlantida*).
11. Paata Burchuladze.
12. *La Bohème.*
13. *La Fanciulla del West,* given by the company's student artists on 4/11/66 to test the acoustics.
14. Giuseppe Taddei.
15. The Met's summer season at Lewisohn Stadium, inaugurated in 1965.

Extra Credit:*

A. *Lohengrin, Die Meistersinger, Tristan und Isolde, Parsifal,* and the four parts of the *Ring.*
B. Anthony A. Bliss, executive director; James Levine, music director; and John Dexter, director of productions.
C. *Pagliacci's* Prologue, *La Bohème* Act I, *Il Barbiere di Siviglia* Act II, and *Aïda* Act I, Scene 1 and Act II.

*One point per opera title (*Ring* and *Aïda,* count a total of four and two, respectively) and one point each per name or company title.

94. ANSWERS

1. *La Traviata.*
2. The Fujiwara Opera Company of Tokyo (the two languages were Italian and Japanese).
3. The 1983 Puccini festival.
4. Phyllis Treigle, daughter of Norman Treigle.
5. *Crispino e lo Comare.*
6. Thea Musgrave, its composer.
7. *Don Giovanni.*
8. *The Tender Land.*
9. Ashley Putnam.
10. *Carmen,* on 10/14/79.
11. 9/2/85.
12. *Silverlake.*
13. The Queen of the Night.
14. The L.A.-based Music Center Opera Association, under whose auspices New York City Opera presented operas in Los Angeles.
15. *La Traviata.*

Extra Credit:*

A. Laszlo Halasz, Joseph Rosenstock, Erich Leinsdorf, Julius Rudel, Beverly Sills, and Christopher Keene.

B. *The Student from Salamanca*/Jan Bach.
Before Breakfast/Thomas Pasatieri.
Madame Adare/Stanley Silverman.

C. *Brigadoon, South Pacific, The Music Man, The Pajama Game,* and *The Sound of Music.*

*One point for each person or opera title.

95. ANSWERS

1. Louise, in *Louise.*
2. Valzacchi.
3. Abe Kaplan.
4. Two nursemaids who have "gone slumming" to the scene of the crime.
5. *Das Tagblatt.*
6. *"In Paris ist Revolution ausgebrochen"* ("Revolution has broken out in Paris").
7. *Of Mice and Men.*
8. Maria Corona.
9. If she kills someone.
10. Dutch.
11. *Constituzional.*
12. *Castoro.*
13. *La Gazetta.*
14. Bill Zakariesen.
15. Hector Berlioz.

Extra Credit:*

The Times, Tribune, Sun, Herald, and *Clipper.*

*One point per correct title.

96. ANSWERS

1. Seventeen
2. Six months
3. Sixteen
4. Eighteen
5. Twelve
6. Twenty-one
7. Forty-seven
8. Twenty
9. Fifteen
10. Fifty
11. Forty-six
12. Thirty-three
13. Eighteen years and two months
14. Ninety
15. Minus eight

Extra Credit:*

A. c
B. d
C. h
D. e
E. f
F. b
G. g
H. a

*One point per answer.

97. ANSWERS

1. Handball.
2. To retrieve their ball, which had been thrown inside.
3. Five.
4. Cleopatra.
5. *Les Troyens.*
6. *Fedora.*
7. Gounod's *Sapho.*
8. Chess.
9. *Death in Venice.*
10. *La Belle Hélène.*

Extra Credit:*

A. Charlie, Joan, and Willie.
B. Barbamuche.
C. Samuel Barber.

*One point for each name in A, two points each for B and C.

98. ANSWERS

1. *Treemonisha.*
2. Crown, in *Porgy and Bess.*
3. Mistletoe.
4. *Rinaldo.*
5. Nika Magadoff.
6. A giant oak tree.
7. By holding onto Mefistofele's cloak.
8. In tea.
9. 70 St. Mary Axe.
10. Taven.
11. Ortrud.
12. A dragon.
13. Lamère Grabille.
14. Le Marquis de Saluces.
15. Alfred Cellier.

Extra Credit:*

A. The Queen of Hearts, the Two of Spades, and the Queen of Hearts again.
B. Three-and-six.
C. A Blessing.

*One point for each of the three draws in A, two points per B and C.

99. ANSWERS

1. Italian.
2. Mattia Battistini.
3. Canadian George London.
4. F sharp, one of the highest notes asked of a soprano in opera.
5. *The Fiery Angel.*
6. Gertrude Stein (composer Gerald Tyrwhitt, who commissioned it, never did write the score).
7. *Bianca und Giuseppe.*
8. Leone Emanuele.
9. Benjamin Franklin.
10. Michael Balfe, composer of *The Bohemian Girl.*

11. *Natoma.*
12. The Manhattan Opera Company, which folded before the work could be produced.
13. Helga Dernesch.
14. Cavaliere di Gran Croce.
15. *Ba-Ta-Clan.*

Extra Credit:*

A. His high D.
B. D
C. C

*Score two points for each answer in the body of the quiz, and four points for each extra credit question.

100. ANSWERS*

1. *Owen Wingrave.*
2. Swan Vestas.
3. *"Celui que j'exercise"* ("The same as mine").
4. The 21st, under Napoleon III.
5. Lulu.
6. *"Matrimonio Presto,"* whose M and P she claims she reads in Dorabella's palm.
7. He has a spatula-mark on his right arm.
8. A girl.
9. *Il Viaggio a Reims.*
10. Vassar.
11. Mardian.
12. *La Princesse Jaune.*
13. *Cox and Box.*
14. *Deseret* (by Leonard Kastle).
15. Capricorn.

Extra Credit:*

A. Regalias, Auroras, and Eurekas.
B. *L'Amico Fritz* and *Le Juif Polonais,* respectively.
C. Edwin and Angelina.

*Two points per answer in the body of the quiz, and two points for each object, work, or name in A, B, and C.

Appendix

WORKS FEATURED IN THIS BOOK

Below, a list of all operas, operettas, and musical comedies contained in *What's Your Opera I.Q.?*

The Abduction of Figaro
Acis and Galatea
L'Africaine
Aïda
L'Aiglon
Akhnaten
Albert Herring
Alceste
Aleko
Alessandro
Amahl and the Night Visitors
Amelia Goes to the Ball
L'Amico Fritz
El Amor Brujo
Amore dei Tre Re
Andrea Chénier
Angélique
Aniara
Anna Bolena
Antony and Cleopatra
Arabella
Ariadne auf Naxos
L'Arianna Abbandonada
Ariodante

Arlecchio
L'Assedio di Corinto
At the Boar's Head
Atlantida
Attila
Atys
Aureliano in Palmira

Babar the Elephant
The Ballad of Baby Doe
Un Ballo in Maschera
Il Barbiere di Siviglia (2)
Barkouf
The Bartered Bride
Ba-Ta-Clan
La Battaglia di Legnano
The Bear
Beatrice di Tenda
Beatrice et Bénédict
Beatrix Cenci
Before Breakfast
The Beggar's Opera
La Belle Hélène
Betrothal in a Monastery

Bianca und Giuseppe
Billy Budd
La Bohème (2)
The Bohemian Girl
Boris Godunov
The Bride from Pluto
Brigadoon

La Calisto
La Campana Sommersa
Candide
Capriccio
Captain Jinks of the Horse Marines
Cardillac
Carmen
Carmina Burana
Carousel
Casanova
Cavalleria Rusticana
Cendrillon
La Cenerentola
Chérubin
Le Cheval de Bronze
Christóbal Colón
Christopher Columbus
Le Cid
La Clemenza di Tito
Les Contes d'Hoffmann
The Consul
Le Convenienze Teatrali
Le Coq d'Or
Il Corsaro
Una Cosa Rara
Così Fan Tutte
Cox and Box
The Cradle Will Rock
The Cricket on the Hearth
Crispino e lo Comare
The Crucible
The Cunning Little Vixen
Die Czárdásfürstin

Dalibor

La Dame Blanche
Daphne
Death in Venice
Deseret
Les Deux Aveugles
The Devil and Daniel Webster
The Devils of London
Le Devin du Village
Dialogues of the Carmelites
Diana of Salange
Dido and Aeneas
Dinorah
Doctor Faustus Lights the Lights
Le Docteur Miracle
Le Docteur Ox
Die Dollarprinzessin
Dom Sebastian
Don Carlo
Don Giovanni
Don Pasquale
Don Procopio
Don Quichotte
Don Rodrigo
Don Sanche
Le Donne Curiose
Die Drei Pintos
Drei Waltzer
Il Due Foscari
Il Due Litiganti
Duke Bluebeard's Castle

L'Eclair
Edgar
Einstein on the Beach
Elegy for Young Lovers
Elektra
Elisabetta di Siberia
Elisabetta, Regina di l'Inghilterra
L'Elisir d'Amore
The Emerald Isle
The Emperor Jones
L'Enfant et les Sortilèges

The English Cat
Die Entführung aus dem Ser-
ail
Ernani
Erwartung
L'Etoile
L'Etoile du Nord
Eugene Onegin
The Excursions of Mr.
Brouvček

Falstaff
La Fanciulla del West
Faust
La Favorita
Fedora
Fidelio
Fierrabras
The Fiery Angel
La Fille du Régiment
La Fille du Tambour-Major
La Finta Giardiniera
Der Fledermaus
Der Fliegende Holländer
Follies
La Forza del Destino
Four Saints in Three Acts
Fra Diavolo
Francesca da Rimini
Frau Luna
Die Frau ohne Schatten
Der Freischütz
The Frogs
From the House of the Dead

Gallantry
The Gambler
La Gazza Ladra
La Gazzetta
Genoveva
Gianni Schicchi
Giants of the Earth
La Gioconda
Un Giorno di Regno

Giulio Cesare
Gloriana
The Gondoliers
Götterdämmerung
La Grande Duchesse de Gérol-
stein
Grisélidis
Il Guarany
Guillaume Tell
Guntram

Halka
A Hand of Bridge
Hänsel und Gretel
Harriet: A Woman Called
Moses
Háry János
Help! Help! The Globolinks!
Henry VIII
L'Heure Espangnole
Higglety Pigglety Pop!
Hin und Zurück
H.M.S. Pinafore
Les Huguenots
Hunyadi László

Idomeneo
L'Incoronzione di Poppea
Les Indes Galantes
Intermezzo
Iphigénie en Tauride
The Island God
L'Italiana in Algeri
Ivan IV
Ivanhoe

Jeanne d'Arc au Bucher
Jenufa
La Jolie Fille de Perth
Le Jongleur de Notre-Dame
Le Juif Polonais
La Juive
Julien
Juliette

The Jumping Frog of Cal-
   averas County
Der Junge Lord
The Juniper Tree

Kátya Kabanová
Khovanshchina
The King Goes Forth to
   France
King Lear
King Priam
King Roger
Kismet
Kiss Me Kate
Konigskinder

Lakmé
The Last Savage
Leonora
The Libertine
Die Liebe der Danae
Das Liebesverbot
A Life for the Tsar
Linda di Chamounix
The Little Sweep
Lizzie Borden
La Loca
Lodoletta
Lohengrin
I Lombardi
Lost in the Stars
Lou Salome
Louise
The Love for Three Oranges
Lucrezia Borgia
Lucia di Lammermoor
Luisa Miller
Lulu
Die Lustige Witwe

Macbeth
Madama Butterfly
Madame Adair

The Making of the Represen-
   tative for Planet 8
The Makropoulos Case
Les Malheurs d'Orphée
Les Mamelles de Tirésias
The Man Who Mistook His
   Wife for a Hat
Manon
Manon Lescaut (2)
Manru
Maria di Rohan
Maria Golovin
Mary Queen of Scots
Maria Stuarda
Martha
Il Matrimonio Segreto
Mavra
Medée
Le Médecin Malgré Lui
The Medium
Mefistofele
Merrily We Roll Along
Merry Mount
The Merry Wives of Windsor
Mesdames de la Halle
A Midsummer Marriage
A Midsummer Night's Dream
The Mighty Casey
Mignon
The Mikado
Minutes Till Midnight
Mireille
Miss Havisham's Fire
Mitridate Eupatore
Mitridate. Re di Ponto
Der Mond
Il Mondo della Luna
Monsieur Choufleuri
Montezuma
Mosé in Egitto
The Most Important Man
The Mother of Us All
The Mountebanks

La Muette de Portici
The Music Man
My Fair Lady

Nabucco
Natoma
Naughty Marietta
New Year
A Night at the Chinese Opera
Nine Rivers from Jordan
Norma
The Nose
Noye's Fludde
Le Nozze di Figaro

L'Oca del Cairo
Oedipus Rex
Of Mice and Men
L'Oiseau Bleu
The Old Maid and the Thief
1000 Airplanes on the Roof
Orfeo ed Euridice
Orlando
Orphée aux Enfers
Otello
Owen Wingrave

Pacific Overtures
Padmâvati
Pagliacci
The Pajama Game
Les Pêcheurs de Perles
The Passion of Jonathan
    Wade
Patience
Paul Bunyan
Pelléas et Mélisande
Pénélope
La Périchole
Peter Grimes
Peter Ibbetson
Philémon et Baucis
Phoebus and Pan
The Pilgrim's Progress

Pique Dame
Il Pirata
The Pirates of Penzance
La Plège de Méduse
La Pomme d'Api
Porgy and Bess
Postcard from Morocco
Le Postillon de Longjumeau
The Postman Always Rings
    Twice
Les Pré aux Clercs
Pince Igor
La Princesse Jaune
I Puritani

I Quattro Rusteghi
A Quiet Place

The Rake's Progress
The Rape of Lucrezia
Rasputin
Regina
La Reine de Saba
Riders to the Sea
Rienzi
Rigoletto
Rinaldo
[The Ring Cycle:
    Götterdämmerung
    Das Rheingold
    Siegfried
    Die Walküre]
Rip Van Winkle
Robert le Diable
Roberto Deveraux
Le Roi de Lahore
Le Roi d'Ys
Le Roi l'A Dit
Le Roi Malgré Lui
Roméo et Juliette
La Rondine
Der Rosenkavalier
Le Rossignol
Ruddigore

Rusalka
Russalka

Sadko
Saint Elizabeth
The Saint of Bleecker Street
Salome
Samson et Dalila
Sapho
Sappho
The Saracen
Satyagraha
Lo Schiavo
Die Schweigsame Frau
Semele
Semiramide
La Serva Padorna
The Seven Deadly Sins
Show Boat
The Siege of Rhodes
Siegfried
Il Signor Bruschino
Silverlake
Simon Boccanegra
Sir John in Love
Six Characters in Search of an Author
Song of Norway
La Sonnambula
The Sorcerer
The Sound of Music
Sous le Masque
South Pacific
The Story of a Real Man
Street Scene
The Student from Salamanca
Summer and Smoke
Suor Angelica
Susanna
Sweeney Todd

Il Tabarro
Tannhäuser
The Temple of Minerva

The Tender Land
The Threepenny Opera
Tosca
Die Tote Stadt
La Tragédie de Carmen
La Traviata
Treemonisha
Trial by Jury
Tristan und Isolde
Troilus and Cressida
Trouble in Tahiti
Troubled Island
Il Trovatore
Les Troyens
The Tsar's Bride
Turandot
Il Turco in Italia
The Turn of the Screw
The Two Widows

Utopia Limited

Vanessa
La Vera Storia
I Vespri Siciliani
La Vestale
Il Viaggio a Reims
La Vie Parisienne
Le Villi
Viola
The Voice of Ariadne
La Voix Humaine
La Voyage dans la Lune

Die Walküre
La Wally
War and Peace
Werther
West Side Story
Where the Wild Things Are
The White Horse Inn
The Wings of a Dove
Wozzeck
Wuthering Heights

X
Xerxes

The Yeomen of the Guard
Yolanta

Zar und Zimmerman
Die Zauberflöte
Zaza
Der Zigeunerbaron
The Zoo
*Zwei Herzen im Dreivier-
teltakt*

About the Author

Iris Bass grew up listening to the Texaco Opera Quiz and its surrounding Metropolitan Opera matinee broadcasts, in that order of interest. One of her earliest opera-related memories is of laughing herself silly over Milton Cross's description of Gilda's murder. Since falling utterly in love with live performance while in her late teens—the turning point was a New York City Opera *Le Coq d'Or*—she has attended hundreds of opera performances in the United States and abroad. She still thinks that business with the sack leaves something to be desired.

A book designer for twelve years, Iris now works in the editorial department of a major paperback publishing house. She is also the designer of *Opera Fanatic* magazine and has appeared as guest on its affiliated radio program on WKCR-FM. Iris is a cofounder of OPERA GLASS, a not-for-profit opera-supportive audience organization incorporated in 1984, and since its inception has been editor of OG's journal, *Sightlines,* in which some of these quizzes made their debut.

Her eclectic operatic tastes have a particular slant toward nineteenth century French works, Rossini, and stratospheric voices. Iris shares her book- and recording-filled Brooklyn apartment with a rambunctious cat who prefers early Verdi and basses. They argue, often.